# The Bridge

## Crossing Over into the Fullness of Covenant Life

## By Tyler Dawn Rosenquist

The Bridge – Crossing Over Into the Fullness of Covenant Life

© 2014 Tyler Dawn Rosenquist

Cover artwork, "Walking in the Light"

© 2014 Darlene Dine

"Salvation is Your Name"

Written and performed by Joshua Aaron, who gave his permission for the song lyrics to be used here. Copyright: © 2006 WorshipinIsrael.com songs

All scripture quotes, unless otherwise noted, are from the King James Version of the Bible.

## Dedication and Special Thanks

This book is dedicated to my beloved husband of 23 years, Mark, and my beautiful children Matthew and Andrew, who taught me 13 years ago that adoption isn't a consolation prize, but instead to be specially handpicked by God from among all the children on earth for a very specific family and a very specific calling. This book is also dedicated to my online brothers and sisters who have labored with me, challenged me, put up with me, taught me, and helped me to grow – and who gave me many suggestions for this book out of love for their brothers and sisters in Messiah. I wouldn't be where I am today without all of you and I love you.

Special thanks to Darlene Dine, my precious sister and the wonderful artist who created the beautiful "Walking in the Light" for the cover. I am privileged to know you and see your work on my wall each morning when I wake up. You daily remind me that I am on a journey of increasing promise and beauty.

Most of all, I thank my Heavenly Father for drawing me, and my Messiah, who took my penalty on the cross. May I someday be found worthy enough to hear "Well done, good and faithful servant."

## Introduction

This isn't intended to be a dry, scholarly trip through the scriptures looking for the reasons why the law of Christ is the law that should govern our lives as believers. I am going to instead first make a case for the character of God and the validity of His Word. I am going to take the familiar concepts that His Word is based on – home, adoption, father/child, king/ambassador, free man/slave, husband/wife, and bridegroom/bride – in order to challenge the concept of our walk with Him as it is commonly taught. Family relationships should neither be cold nor lukewarm, but the reality of our lives here on earth is far different from the perfection that was meant to be. We are raised in flawed families by flawed people, and many of those families have left God's people with a twisted idea of what the words father/child, home, husband/wife, and bridegroom/bride should look like in the Divine setting. And culturally in most of the western world, we no longer understand the ancient concepts of king/ambassador, or free man/slave either. I want to change that for you – because you were always meant to understand those relationships based on love and loyalty and covenant. You deserve to experience the restoration of that kind of understanding.

I am not actually going to tell you anything you don't already know, deep down in your heart and mind. I am not going to tell you anything that the Spirit hasn't been telling you for a long time about God the Father, and Jesus, and the Word. It's just been so buried under the teachings we grew up with, both culturally and religiously, that you didn't even realize that you knew them. It will all make sense if you give me your time and patience. It will be a bit foreign, because of where and how we grew up – far from the culture of the Bible, but some things are eternal. You just need a bridge to cross over on, from our culture, to God's culture. I pray this book can be your bridge.

## Something's Wrong

Who am I? I'm no one very important, apart from being your sister in Messiah, my freedom bought by the same blood that bought your freedom. My expectation of the resurrection from the dead is the same as yours; my Heavenly Father is the same as your Heavenly Father. My Bible is the same as your Bible. The Spirit I am filled with is the same Spirit that you are filled with. I want to please God and you want to please God. We both want to hear the words, "Well done, good and faithful servant." So that, in a nutshell, is who I am. And I pray that, even if you disagree with some of the things that I might write, that you would see me as I see you, as living stones of the temple of God. What I laid out are the things which unite us, and I believe they are greater than any doctrinal divisions. In my mind, there is nothing greater than Messiah and Him crucified, risen and returning! If we agree on that, then we agree on the most important things that exists and everything else can be sorted out accordingly. If we can love and respect each other based upon those truths, then we have a foundation to build a relationship upon.

What's really important to me is who you are – and if you're anything like me, then you know something's wrong but you might not know exactly what it is. People might be telling you to ignore your misgivings and "just pray," but prayer only intensifies the feeling that something isn't quite right. They tell you to read your Bible – but reading your Bible is how you got your doubts in the first place. They tell you to go to Church more often, but that doesn't work – or maybe you have already left. You want to know how the first century church worked so many miracles – but maybe what you really want to know most is "why do I feel so uneasy when I am trying so hard to be faithful?" Why, when you are trying so diligently to get things right, have things sometimes gone so wrong since becoming a believer? Why have your blessings been withheld when things seem to go so right for others? Why did so many

3

things seem to fall apart when you accepted Jesus as your Savior, even as other things started to go right? Why don't you have any real inner assurance that you are truly living in a way that makes God happy?

The good news (no pun intended) is that there is no problem with Jesus, the only begotten Son of God who died so that our sins would be forgiven. He is the true Messiah of Israel, don't ever believe otherwise. The problem is that when you surrendered your life to Him, you signed on to a Covenant confirmed by His righteous blood, and no one told you how to hold up your end of the bargain. In fact, they told you that it was faithlessness, and a sin, to read the fine print and do what was required of you in order to walk in the fullness of blessings. They told you that He did it all and you don't have to do anything – except what they want you to do, and they all have things they want you to do, promising that if you do things their way, that the blessings will come. But the blessings they promised haven't come, and maybe you are tired of them treating you as though your life would be easy if you would just do things their way. I don't blame you for living that way and I really don't blame the people who taught you that either, because it's just what they were taught and maybe they didn't really question it – but this isn't about blame, this is about getting things right and moving forward. There isn't any time to look back in anger or resentment or even regret. It's time to learn the truth and rejoice.

And if you go forward rejoicing about the truth instead of angry about the lies, you are going to save yourself a lot of time that I wasted. God has so much He wants for you, a way of life He chose that pleases Him, and He always meant for you to be a part of it, before you were knit together in your mother's womb.

So if you are anything like I was, and you know something is wrong – will you travel with me a little while? I want to strengthen your faith in the Messiah of Israel, I want to show you how incredibly faithful and fair

4

and unchanging our Heavenly Father is, and I want to show you how you can live according to the way you were probably taught was impossible, through the power of the Holy Spirit – having the inner assurance that you are pleasing to God and not just hoping. I want to explore the nature of love, grace and faith with you.

But more than anything, I want to teach you how God created you to live in cooperation with Him like a little child with their Father, how to truly make Him the Master of your life, how to become a beautiful bride for the Bridegroom, and how to be a faithful ambassador to the King of Kings.

Are you desperate enough to try something radical? Are you desperate enough to follow a rejected, first century, supposedly illegitimate, itinerant Jewish Rabbi who died in disgrace alongside criminals? Are you foolish enough, in the world's eyes, to cling to someone like that? Would you have opened this book if you weren't?

## The Dilemma

Everyone is aware on some level that we have a crisis on our hands. And before we were believers we saw it very clearly – Christianity isn't practicing what it preaches. Before we had a personal revelation of Jesus as Messiah (if we came into the faith as adults), it really offended us. But then we got on the inside, and we decided we had been all wrong. Year after year, though, it got harder and harder to ignore what we once saw with such clarity.

Once upon a time, we realized that we needed a Savior because we weren't living up to God's standards – but once we became part of the family, we were told that some of those standards were gone for us, and that they only applied to outsiders. But how can that be? Can sin stop being sin? Is it okay to sin if someone died to take our penalty? Would we say that if our mom confessed to our crimes and took our prison sentence? Would we say that the laws that put her behind bars no longer applied to us? Or would we be so grateful that mom bailed us out that we would confess and work to turn our lives around, if we were truly repentant?

We were sold a bill of goods. We were told that once our penalty was paid for by someone else – that we could break the law again and it would be okay, as long as our denomination approves of the law being broken. Imagine being freed from being grounded only to tell our parents that their rules no longer applied to us because they had freed us from the consequence. If that reasoning wouldn't work in a flawed human family, why on earth would we accept it as part of a divine family?

The truth is that the very laws that convicted us of our sins and sent us to our knees in the first place, are the same laws that were meant to teach us how to live as part of God's eternal family. They are the house rules of a loving Father. They teach us how to love the LORD and love one another, they teach us that there is a way we can know we are pleasing Him – so that we don't have to just hope we will be considered good and faithful servants in the end. These laws are no different than we see in any family on earth – defining the things we do and do not celebrate, do and do not eat, do and do not wear, how to be safe, how to keep from doing wrong and how to make up for it when we do. Far from being legalistic or too difficult, it's really just a lifestyle change, an "eternal life" –style change. But I don't want you to take my word for it. I am going to let Jesus, Moses and Paul prove it to you, in their own words, in context.

If you were a child who had been adopted by an American family and came to the United States from a different country, you would be subject to the rules and culture of that family. Although eating dogs, cats, or horses might be perfectly acceptable where you came from – to an American it is detestable. You would give up certain celebrations of your culture, and adopt new ones. Things that were tolerated where you came from might now be taboo – and if you were used to doing those things, you might call your new mom and dad legalistic for not allowing you to continue to do them. But you wouldn't be right, because within a cultural context, their rules are perfectly reasonable and are not depriving you of anything you need to be healthy and survive.

God has a culture too, one that is found in the pages of the Bible – from the writings of Moses to the Gospels, all the way to Revelation. God, as our adoptive parent, has expectations for how we are to live happy, productive, and healthy lives in harmony with His other children. He expects us to learn to love and care about the things He loves and cares about. Jesus, the Messiah of Israel, lived that life – and so did all of his disciples, as I will prove throughout this book. Apart from Jesus, none of them were perfect people, but they lived lives pleasing to God because they strove to do things His way.  They understood what it is to have a perfect Father, whose rules were not tyrannical but instead beneficial.

Too many of us were taught to look at God the Father in a way that Jesus never presented Him.  Wouldn't you like to be introduced to the Father that Jesus actually preached?

I hope so.

## The Perfect Dad

When Jesus says that someone is a good Father, wouldn't we believe Him? I mean, wouldn't that be like the gold seal of approval? When Jesus says that the Father knows how to give good gifts, wouldn't we know for sure that the gifts are good?[1] When Jesus says that the doctrine He is preaching is His Father's doctrine,[2] don't we know then – that because Jesus is good, and the Father is good, that the doctrine is good? And by good, I mean perfect, not even a hint of evil.

So why have we been taught that the doctrine of the Father is flawed? Did Jesus teach that? Did Jesus teach that God the Father gave His chosen people, the Israelites, an impossible way to live just to prove that they couldn't do it and then punish them for it? We have to really think about this – right before the end of the first Temple period, there were parents reduced to eating their own children during the lengthy siege of Jerusalem, people being slaughtered by the Babylonians, women raped and babies being dashed against rocks. Was this the wrathful punishment for not being able to keep a Father's impossible standards? Or were these the consequences against a nation for not even trying anymore and effectively leaving their Father's house in favor of worshipping other gods, and therefore His protection – just like the prodigal son in Jesus' parable, who left his father's house to enjoy the pleasures of sin for a season, only to find starvation and homelessness far from the protection and bounty of his loving family.

The children of Israel, far from being unable to live according to the Torah,[3] the instructions of God found recorded in the five books of

---

[1] Matt 7:11, Luke 11:13, all scripture quoted from the King James Version unless otherwise noted

[2] John 7:16

[3] The word Torah is translated as "law" 291 times in the Hebrew Bible, the Tanakh, called the Old Testament by Christians. First mentioned in Gen 26:5 as

Moses, did in fact live by it during certain eras, eras marked by incredible peace and prosperity. It was only during the times when they did things their own way that they got into trouble. The entire Book of Judges (as well as I and II Kings and I and II Chronicles) details this struggle between righteous and sinful living as a nation. During the times that they lived in harmony with God, they were incredibly blessed, and during those times when they lived in defiant rebellion, they were incredibly cursed. The prophetic books were not written during the blessed times, but during the rebellious years of curses.

Isn't it the same in our homes? When everyone obeys the rules, there is peace in the home and it is a joy to live with one another. But when people live in opposition, it is nothing less than torture. If our rules, as parents, bring peace to our home – how much more amazing would the house rules designed by God be? Can a good God create bad rules? Can a loving God create hateful standards? Can the Father who Jesus preached, if Jesus is truthful, create an impossible system and then punish those who cannot, by definition, ever measure up?

I submit that not only is Jesus truthful, He is the truth. He is the way and He is also the life.[4] And that life is the light of men.[5] And He is the very seen image of His unseen Father.[6] For many years we have been seeing Father and Son as two distinct entities, but that isn't entirely true – because two entities, no matter how close they are, will never agree on everything. But the Father and Son are One, Echad,[7] in everything. If it were not so, then only one and not the other would be perfect, or perhaps neither would be. But I submit that scripture can only support

---

being the instructions that Abraham obeyed and was blessed because of (begin in verse 4)
[4] John 14:6
[5] John 1:4
[6] Col 1:15
[7] John 10:30

the position that both Father and Son are absolutely perfect, and therefore absolutely unchanging – after all, to change perfection would by definition result in imperfection.  To change perfection – would require rebellion.

## The Rebellious or Dutiful Son?

No one says it in so many words, but Jesus is painted to be quite the rebel towards His Father. I'm going to let you in on a little secret – Jesus is the perfect Son, always obedient, always working within His Father's commandments, always respecting and promoting them. And might I add that because Jesus is perfect and perfectly good, if His Father's commandments were not perfectly good, He would be unable to keep them – it would be against His very nature to do so.

But Jesus was also a rebel, just never towards His Father. Although to be fair, one can really only rebel against those who have legitimate authority in your life. There were many in His day who claimed legitimate authority given by God and no, they weren't called Pharisees, who were simply members of a small denomination (less than 5,000 members) within Judaism, known as Orthodox in our modern times – these authorities were called scribes, teachers, and rabbis. Unfortunately, religion in Jesus' day was no different than religion in our day – and men took it upon themselves to add to and subtract from the laws of God, just like we have seen in the churches for almost 2000 years now. Jesus was often at odds with some these men, who criticized people for not keeping their laws regarding the ritual washing of hands, tables and pots,[8] and their laws that made Sabbath difficult to observe, laws that said you could not make mud with your spit, carry a bedroll or pick heads of grain to eat on the seventh day.[9] You see, they made those laws up; they extrapolated them from existing commandments, often taking them completely out of context to do it, and had no right to judge people for not keeping them. They had a right to choose and live by those laws if they wanted to, but they had no right to elevate them to equal or greater standing than the laws of the LORD

---

[8] Mark 7:8

[9] Mishnah Tractate Shabbat 7:2 contains 39 categories of prohibitions designed to keep people from doing anything that might lead to work.

written in the Bible and impose them on others – and that was what they were doing, breaking Deuteronomy 4:2 and 12:32 – which forbade anyone from adding to or subtracting from the laws the LORD gave to Moses for the conduct of His children.

Jesus' challenges made some of the religious leaders very angry, and perhaps your questions have made your religious leaders angry – maybe you can relate! There were a few reasons they wanted to kill Him, but one of the main ones was that his teachings were stripping them of their authority to have power over the people based on the traditions of the elders,[10] the laws that had been created by men. When Jesus came against some of these laws, it was a direct attack on their claim that their relationship with God gave them the absolute right to make new laws for the people to follow. Starting shortly after the time of Joshua, the Israelites would often kill the prophets who were sent to remind the people that only the LORD Himself was allowed to make laws by which people could be judged. And over the last 1900 years, we have seen this same thing in Christianity as well – as many saints have lost their lives protesting the edicts of the churches and calling them an affront on the very authority of God the Father and His Messiah, Jesus. Many men and women have died as martyrs in defense of the authority that belongs to God and God alone – no wonder Jesus commanded that we call no man father![11] The father sets the rules for the children, and so as members of the family of God, only God can set the rules. When we call someone else Father, we are setting them into a place of authority, and that can be incredibly dangerous. We must remember that Jesus always, always deferred to the will of the Father, even to death.[12] If we follow Him, then that is the example we must follow.

---

[10] Matt 15:2, Mark 7:3, 7:5
[11] Matt 23:9
[12] Phil 2:8

## A Matter of Loyalty

Now, I am not arguing for a monarchy in this day and age, where we have a human line of kings and queens – but the truth is that we really miss a lot of what the Bible teaches us when we do not properly understand what it is to have a King, and to be the representative or servant of a King.  We no longer live within the context of the absolute loyalty that subjects were required to display, and the penalties for treachery.  The rights of a King were pretty much absolute in many areas of the world not so very long ago, unlike the modern day monarchies where often the title is simply traditional, conferring only honorary status.

In the ancient world, even 500 years ago, to be the subject of a King meant you understood the rights of that King to make laws and to command absolute obedience from his subjects. In addition, there would also be an understanding of the absolute protection from foreign powers that a King owed to his subjects.  An ambassador of the King could never act of his own authority, would never speak ill of his King, nor betray his King unless he wanted to be found guilty of treason and summarily executed.  Nor would the ambassador, if he was a faithful servant, sit by idly while his King was being defamed or plotted against. No, it was the job of the ambassador to promote the Kingship, to honor him and promote his honor before the world, to be unquestioningly faithful and loyal, and to always, in his every action, work and speak towards the benefit of his Kingdom.

A good ambassador would never compromise his King's principles.

A good ambassador would never openly question nor disobey his King's commands.

A good ambassador would never go to work trying to establish his own power base at the expense of his King's authority and dominion.

A good ambassador would never seek out anything but the welfare of his King's people.

A good ambassador would never act in a way that would bring shame to his King.

A good ambassador would never add to or subtract from the messages sent forth by his King.

Can you imagine, thousands of years ago, any ambassador of a Caesar or Pharaoh, taking their king's sealed messages, opening them up, and adding to or subtracting from what they found there? If the Caesars and Pharaohs, in their human limitations and depravity, commanded such loyalty and absolute respect in the treatment of their words, how much more respect do we owe our righteous and eternal LORD?

We no longer have earthly Kings, in most areas of the world, with the authority over our life and death – but we do have an eternal King with the authority over our life and death. The problem is, we don't act like it and in our honest moments, we have to admit that we really don't treat Him very seriously. Historically, even bad monarchs were seen as the hope of their people, the source of blessings and curses, and were taken very seriously. If one's land was being invaded, they looked to the King for their salvation. If there was a problem or a crime, they looked to their King for justice. If there was a question of right or wrong, they looked to the King's laws to define it. And people would follow those laws, and render the proper respect to their King in all matters.

If you were a good King, and you had before you a group of your servants, and you were going to reward them based on how they served you, to whom would you say, "Well done, good and faithful servant?"[13]

---

[13] Matt 25:21, 23; Luke 19:17

Would it be to the ones who thought good thoughts about you, who sat in a room a few times a week and said nice things about you, sang about you, and did good deeds in your name, but did it all according to their own best judgment? Or –

Would you say it to those who did exactly what you told them to do, to the best of their ability, and came to you and admitted when they fell short, who never questioned your orders, or went off and did things another way that they thought was better, or ignored your orders all together, or called them outdated and unreasonable and told others that as well? And all this while, like the first group, praising you publicly and doing good deeds in your name.

Who is the good and faithful servant? In your own life, what kind of servant would you desire? The one who is unquestioningly obedient and trusting in your wisdom, or the one who does what they want, how they want – in your name?

It's about loyalty. It's about the credit we give our eternal King, in our thoughts and actions, for being fair and perfect in all His dealings. Human monarchs can make bad, unjust, unreasonable laws, but by definition – God is incapable of it. At least, the God Jesus preached is incapable of it. I believe everything that Jesus ever said. I believe with perfect faith that Jesus Christ is our Master and coming King, the Lion of Judah, Messiah son of David, the perfect representation of the Father in Heaven.

And I believe that God the Father, by extension, is absolutely just and fair and eternally consistent in His dealings.

## Serving a Proverbs 11:1 King

One of the great underlying themes of the Bible, from the first page to the last, is justice and fairness.

*Pro 11:1 (KJV) A false balance is abomination to the LORD: but a just weight is his delight.*

We serve a great God incapable of breaking His own laws, by virtue of His excellent character, because as John said, transgression of the law is sin.[14]  Do I have to establish that our God is sinless?  No, I didn't think so, I would be preaching to the proverbial choir!  There are laws forbidding injustice,[15] commanding that we hold everyone, from foreigner to priest, to the same standards.  Neither rich, nor poor, nor citizen, nor foreigner, nor widow, nor orphan... you get the idea – is to be held to a different standard than anyone else.  It is actually a commandment not to show favoritism, to anyone, and is echoed by the apostle Paul as well![16]  Show me another god worshiped on this planet with a rule like that!  And because we know that God does not sin, He shows no favoritism either.  I know this is going to be hard to believe, because yes, the Jews are God's chosen people to bring forth the Messiah and preserve the oracles of God, but His favor towards them is not the same as favoritism.  It's about something we have very little modern understanding of – Covenant promises, and the advantages and liabilities that go along with them.  I will go into that later.

Did you know that one never had to be a native born Israelite to be a full citizen of God's people?  Did you know that when the Israelites were taken out of Egypt, a whole lot of Gentiles went along with them?[17]  Can you blame them?  Egypt had been devastated by plagues at the hand of

---

[14] I John 3:4
[15] Ex 12:49, Lev 24:22, Num 9:14, 15:15-16, 29-30
[16] Gal 3:28; Col 3:11
[17] Ex 12:38

this powerful God, and I should imagine that people from every walk of life – slave to noble – were among what the Bible called the "mixed multitude" that left Egypt. Their "gods" had been dishonored by the LORD, one by one, and so the most natural thing in the world was to follow after the victorious God.

At Mt Sinai, when the LORD called down His commandments, they were the same for the descendants of Jacob as they were for the mixed multitude – and in fact, He went out of His way to say it several times.[18] Was it a warning to the people not to try and establish any sort of racially based class system? Of course it was, but as is the case with everything written in the Bible, nothing is there casually. He was also communicating the larger message that He doesn't play favorites, nor is He a respecter of genealogies – apart from the role they play in the fulfillment of prophecy in accordance with specific promises. The children from the line of Jacob were held to the exact same legal status in God's Kingdom, as were the former pagans who fled Egypt to serve this new, to their thinking, God. Anything else would be unfair.

Many people grew up in homes where the rules were not fair, and maybe there was a favorite child who was held to different standards, while the others were treated strictly or perhaps not loved at all. In such a family, the children will forever be at war, laden with resentment. We see this biblically in the accounts of Jacob and Esau, and Joseph and his brothers, and in the way King David treated his own sons, and daughter.[19] Unrighteous standards among children tear the bonds of brotherhood into shreds. They are the epitome of false balances and inaccurate weights, and the parents who employ them never have the full confidence of their children. Accurate weights are about placing an equal value and equal expectation on each and every person, regardless of personal prejudices. And if God has different

---

[18] Ex 12:49, Num 9:14
[19] Gen 25:28, Gen 37:3, 2 Samuel 13

standards for different people in His Kingdom based on race, then He has committed an abomination, or He changes, which would make Him a liar according to the Prophet Malachi.

*Mal 3:6a For I am the LORD, I change not*

But now we have a problem, because we have been taught that the laws of God were for the Jews and not for Christians – which would require God to commit an abomination in His own eyes. He would have to be going back on His word that any foreigner of the Nations who joins himself to the Kingdom of God is to be held to the same standards. As John said, to transgress the law is sin – does God's character allow Him to sin? What do we really believe about Him?

Maybe our focus has been nudged gradually away from where it was supposed to be.

## The Difference Between Jew, Gentile and Israelite

Definitions define our perceptions, and so it is important that our understanding of words and concepts line up with the Bible and not with the culture and traditions we grew up in.

If I say "January," and you live in most of the Northern Hemisphere, you are going to think "cold." But if you live in the majority of the Southern Hemisphere, you are going to think "warm." Who is correct? Both are. When I talk about having picnics, I am thinking about July but my friends in South Africa are thinking about January! Context is everything. But if you were brought up relatively secluded in the backwoods of Minnesota, it would be unthinkable to imagine someone trekking to the shores of Lake Superior with a basket in hand, wearing flip flops during a month that to you means winter – and so if someone wrote about putting on a swimsuit and going on an outdoor picnic in January you would assume they were insane or that it was a typo. The deal is, not everything happens according to our cultural mindset and we have to make allowances in our mind for that – we have to question every single assumption we make about people who are separated from us by time, language, geography and culture.

And we must especially question ourselves when those assumptions are about the Bible and concern the life and way of thinking of those in first century Israel. There is almost nothing more crucial in this life than understanding what our Messiah was talking about, can we agree on that?

When the Bible uses the terms Jew, Gentile and Israelite, it generally means something different than we do. This is how I was brought up to understand it.

Jew – a descendant of Abraham, through Isaac and Jacob, who keeps the Torah laws and does not believe that Jesus is the Messiah, or who does not keep the Torah laws and is only a Jew by birth.

Gentile – anyone who is not a Jew.

Israelite – Jew.

Spiritual Israelite – Christian.

But how does the Bible define these same terms?

Jew – in general, a Jew was a descendant of Abraham through Isaac, Jacob and his fourth son **Judah**. First mention occurs in 2 Kings 16:6, roughly 740 BC, referring to the citizens of the Southern Kingdom of Judah following the split from the Northern Kingdom of Israel after Solomon's death 200 years earlier. A people group made up mostly of the tribe of Judah, but also Benjamin, and the Levites as well as a remnant that fled the idolatry that King Jeroboam imposed on the Northern Kingdom.[20] During the time of Christ, the term Jew was a generic term for those who had returned from Babylonian exile, who were worshiping the God of Israel. This designation also included those former Gentiles who had converted from paganism to the religion of Judaism (as evidenced by baptism and circumcision with an agreement to follow the specific denominational teachings of their chosen sect). Jesus and all of His disciples and early followers were Jews, for at least a decade after His resurrection.

Gentiles – those of the Nations who were not Jews by birth or conversion. By definition, a Gentile is a person outside of the covenant

---

[20] 1 Kings 12:26-33

promises of God, one who has not made the God of Israel their sovereign (which I will prove in a later chapter).[21]

Israelite (1) – Descendant of Abraham through Isaac and Jacob (called Israel).[22] At Mt Sinai, this was expanded to include those of the mixed multitude who came into Covenant with the God of Israel circa 1446 BC.

Israelite (2) – Citizen of the Northern Kingdom of Israel, with its capital city of Samaria, after the death of Solomon in roughly 931 BC. They largely rejected the Covenants of the God of Israel and turned to idol worship, mixing the biblical standards with the pagan practices of the nations around them. God formally recognized their rejection of the Covenant through the prophets[23] and they incurred the promised curses[24] – war with and exile by the Assyrian Empire in 722 BC. Also called Jacob, Ephraim, or Joseph, these descendants of the 10 northern tribes disappeared into the nations even though they were the genetic descendants of Jacob and were cut off from the Covenant. According to the prophet Ezekiel, Israel (Ephraim) will come back to life again as a people and will be united with Judah, the Jews.[25] Note: there is no scriptural justification for the belief that Christianity constitutes Ephraim, which is a common form of replacement as well as predestination theology, the belief that those who are Christians are automatically descended from the exiled and lost tribes of Israel. This would stand in the face of the fact that at Mt Sinai, many joined themselves to Israel who were not descended from Abraham, Isaac and Jacob.

Israelite (3) – The children of God who are part of the prophesied regathering of the exiles, both Jew and those from the Northern

---

[21] Ephesians 2:11-19
[22] Gen 32:28
[23] Is 50:1, Jer 3:8
[24] Deut 28 and 29
[25] Ezekiel 37, entire chapter, especially 16-28

Kingdom, plus the ingathering of the (former) Gentiles into full covenant status – through the completed work of Messiah in making a way for all who desire to come into Covenant.

Spiritual Israelite – is never mentioned in the Bible.

Isn't that amazing – all our lives we have been taught that we are "spiritual Israel" and the phrase doesn't even exist! I don't know about anyone else, but I want to be defined Biblically, I want to know how my God sees me. I want to know what He says, and not just what people say. All my life I assumed that Spiritual Israel was something scriptural, but it isn't – in truth, what the scriptures say we are is so much better.

I pray you are ready for your heart to start singing! Because that is what mine did when I found out who I am.

## So Are You Implying That I Am Supposed To Be A Jew?

This is a very common question, and the answer is no.  You are a Jew if you were born a Jew or formally converted to religious Judaism, and Judaism in turn is subdivided into those Jews who do and do not believe that Jesus is the Messiah of Israel.  But if you are like me, you were born a Gentile – just like Caleb, Rahab, and Ruth as well as Abraham and Noah.  To be a Gentile, by definition, simply means that we were not born a part of the Covenant made between the LORD and the people of Israel at Mt Sinai.  But the good news is this -- that we were indeed born *to become* a part of the Covenant between the LORD and the people at Mt Sinai.  We were born with every bit as much right to worship the God of Abraham, Isaac and Jacob as anyone else, just as much potential to serve and please Him, and we were born with every bit as much right to claim the Covenant promises and obligations as anyone else.  Remember how I said that God doesn't have different rules for the different people in His Kingdom?  That He is the God of fairness and justice?

Being a Jew has its advantages, just like Paul told the Romans[26] – they are raised with an understanding of the Covenant; they live out God's laws, and they know the Word of God.  But in the end, Jew and Gentile are held to the same exact standards – acceptance of the Messiahship of Jesus, Who was preached throughout the Torah and the Prophets.

There are some who preach that the Jews are saved through the law and the Christians through Jesus, but that isn't fair.  That doesn't reflect the accurate weights that the LORD loves and governs by.  That would somehow say that He has one group of kids whom He treats very strictly, and another group of kids whom He lets do whatever they want as long as they believe all the right things.  The LORD never changes, and so neither do His ways change.  We are either His, or we aren't.  His

---

[26] Ro 3:1-2

standards are either for everyone for all time, or they are subject to alteration when He feels like it. God passionately loves the Jewish people, and would never treat them unfairly. He will keep all of His promises, to them as well as to the Gentiles who become grafted in to His nation.[27]

Part of the confusion is that when Christians look at religious Jews, they see them doing things that look incredibly hard to live by. And it is true – if you weren't raised as an observant tenant of rabbinic Judaism, it is incredibly burdensome. Even if you were raised that way, it can be very difficult. And we were never meant to have such burdens enforced on us as though they were laws from the mouth of God. But we see that, and we assume it is Biblical, and indeed we were taught that it was Biblical, and so it can be a very bad witness as to what the laws of God, as written down by Moses in our Bibles, really do and do not say. It comes down to tradition, and most of what people think of when they think of Jewish observances boil down to traditions of men and not commands from the mouth of God. But we often don't know the difference, we just assume that all those things they do are God's will when truly, in comparison, what is written requires very little of us.

What we commonly associate with modern Judaism sometimes has very little to do with the commandments given by God at Sinai, as I will show throughout this book. Just like the doctrines of Catholicism and Protestantism often have very little to do with what Jesus actually commanded. But like the Jews, our waters have been muddied for thousands of years and we don't always know where to place that dividing line between truth and tradition. You have a choice – to continue in the tradition, or to do what Jesus challenged people to do –

---

[27] Ro 11:17-18

find out what the commandments really are, do them and teach others to do the same.[28]

---

[28] Matt 5:19

## What Did Every Prophet Have in Common?

Biblical prophets had a specific job – and it wasn't telling the future. I know, right? It shocked me too. Biblical prophets had the job of preaching God's commandments to the rebellious, calling them to repentance and pointing them to the Good News. Yes, they also spoke prophecies, but that wasn't their main job. They were the voice of God crying out to the people to come to their senses, remember their Covenant with God, and cooperate with Him in order to enter into blessings again. God has been using prophets to call out to His prodigal children for a long time.

Remember how I talked about God as Father? The prophets would arise most notably during times of rebellion and disobedience, telling God's people to turn from their wickedness, or else! What do good fathers do when their kids are acting wickedly? Tell them to turn away from their wickedness, or else! As parents, we remind our children of the rules of the house, what is and is not acceptable, safe, kind, and moral – and give them an ultimatum. Get your life on the right track OR ELSE. Or else there will be consequences – first at the hands of the parents, but after a while the parents will have to get out of the way and allow society and nature to take care of the "or else." This is what good parents do, hold their children accountable to what is right and discipline them when they fall short. When parents don't do this, we call them rotten parents!

A child who is disobedient is probably not going to have a good adult life. It's just a fact, unless they later turn their lives around. A child who eats junk food is going to be sicker and fatter than one who actually eats things that are nutritious. A child who takes drugs is going to spiral out of control. A child who has sex outside of marriage will be subject to disease and tragedy and will often turn to murdering their own unborn child if there is an unwelcome pregnancy. A person who steals will end up in prison. A person who lies will destroy lives. A person who doesn't respect the rules of the parent, who they are supposed to love, will never be able to respect the rules of those whom they do not love.

The prophets were sent out to the people, the nation of Israel, sometimes with gentle reminders and sometimes yelling, to come back to the rules of the house, or else. But in their warnings was always one thing – the gospel, the good news. And the good news was always the same – from Moses who preached it, to Jesus and His disciples. So what was that good news?

## The Gospel of the Kingdom

I was taught to believe that the Gospel was the death, burial and resurrection of Jesus. Imagine my shock when someone pointed this out – the preaching of the Gospel is mentioned 13 times **before** the death, burial and resurrection of Jesus. Not only did Jesus preach it, but so did His disciples. And we know for a fact that they were clueless that He was going to die. They openly believed that He was coming as Messiah ben[29] David, the prophesied King who they believed would overthrow the Romans. They had no idea He was coming first to die as Messiah ben Joseph, the suffering servant of Isaiah 52 and 53 – so they could not have been preaching that. But they were certainly preaching something – something that the common people loved and some (not all) of the religious leaders hated.

We see the phrase "good news" mentioned by the prophet Isaiah, later quoted by Jesus in the synagogue:

*61:1 The Spirit of the Lord GOD is upon me; because the LORD hath anointed me to preach **good tidings** unto the meek; he hath sent me to bind up the brokenhearted, to proclaim liberty to the captives, and the opening of the prison to them that are bound;*

A sign of the Messiah would be the preaching of the "good news" or gospel. If the people could not identify the good news by its content, they would not be able to identify the Messiah when He preached it. The preaching of the gospel is also associated with binding up the broken hearted, proclaiming liberty to the captives, and the opening of the prison to those who are bound.

Nothing in scripture stands by itself; we must always look back for parallels – and who was associated with being broken-hearted, in

---

[29] Ben is the Hebrew word for son, so ben David means "son of (King) David"

captivity and in prison?  The children of Israel who were suffering under the bondage of slavery in Egypt!  Moses came in the Name of the LORD and preached their release, the opening of the prison and the end to their heartbreak – which the LORD most definitely delivered on.  His salvation of the children of Israel culminated in the experience at Mt Sinai when the laws were given to Moses.  The first law being, "I am the LORD thy God, who brought thee out of bondage in the land of Egypt, thou shall have no other gods before me."[30]  The LORD ended their heartbreak, proclaimed their freedom and let them out of prison.  And then we were taught to believe that He led them right back into bondage with His laws.

Wait a minute!  The LORD brought them out of bondage and into freedom – He promised it and He delivered.  Were they free or not? Or were they now just slaves to another master?  I submit that they were free men, free to enter into an everlasting covenant with the Creator of the universe -- a Covenant which they wholeheartedly agreed to obey.[31]

What was the gospel that was preached at Sinai?

*Hebrews 3:7-4:2 "Wherefore (as the Holy Ghost says, Today if ye will hear his voice, Harden not your hearts, as in the provocation, in the day of temptation in the wilderness: When your fathers tempted me, proved me, and saw my works forty years. Wherefore I was grieved with that generation, and said, They do always err in their heart; and they have not known my ways. So I swore in my wrath, They shall not enter into my rest.) Take heed, brethren, lest there be in any of you an evil heart of unbelief, in departing from the living God. But exhort one another daily, while it is called Today; lest any of you be hardened through the deceitfulness of sin. For we are made partakers of Christ, if we hold the beginning of our confidence steadfast unto the end; While it is said,*

---

[30] Ex 20:2
[31] Ex 19:8

*Today if ye will hear his voice, harden not your hearts, as in the provocation. For some, when they had heard, did provoke: howbeit not all that came out of Egypt by Moses. But with whom was he grieved forty years? Was it not with them that had sinned, whose carcasses fell in the wilderness? And to whom swore he that they should not enter into his rest, but to them that believed not? So we see that they could not enter in because of unbelief. Let us therefore fear, lest, a promise being left us of entering into his rest, any of you should seem to come short of it.*

**For unto us was the gospel preached, <u>as well as unto them</u>: but the word preached did not profit them, not being mixed with faith in them that heard it."**

Whatever that gospel was, it was met with hardened hearts in order to provoke and tempt God. Some did not believe it, and thus departed from God. What is the Gospel? The Gospel has always been God's promised redemption for the purpose of creating a people for Himself. Time and time again, the prophets have preached redemption and deliverance - from Egypt, from Babylon, from sin, from death. The Gospel is good news, and Moses preached it at Sinai, their redemption from Egyptian slavery into right relationship through the Covenant. Jeremiah preached it to the Jews, that the people would be redeemed from Babylon and brought back into right relationship through the Covenant.[32] Hosea preached it to the rebellious house of Israel, that there would someday be a way for redemption and restoration through the Covenant.[33] Jesus and His disciples preached it to the Jews, that a redemption and restoration through the Covenant was coming to the lost sheep of Israel, who as we have seen, had been divorced and exiled

---

[32] Jer 29:10
[33] Hosea 14

for violating that Covenant and needed restoration.[34] The prophets preached of a redemption and restoration that was coming in the millennial reign of Messiah.[35] Redemption and a return to a right relationship with God has always been the good news – eagerly anticipated and longed for since the fall of our common father and mother in the Garden of Eden.

And yet, they sinned against the message through disobedience. So what happened? Namely, God redeemed them and then told them to do something that would lead to blessing, which required obedience, and they refused to do it, an act of rebellion. They had the audacity to decide that His commandments were optional, and so they did not enter into His promises – even after seeing the plagues of Egypt and the Red Sea part and the mountain covered with fire. They did it at Sinai with the Golden Calf right after the first Ten Commandments were given,[36] they did it again when ten of the spies brought an evil report and the people refused to go into the Land,[37] and then again when they whored with the pagan women![38] They did not treat God like He was God. They violated the very word and spirit of the Covenant.

They did not treat the LORD like He was their Lord and Master. They treated the Covenant and God with contempt. God's commandments and His Covenant with us are good news, because they alone show us the path to live in harmony and cooperation with the all-wise, all-loving, all-powerful God of Creation, and with each other. What on earth could possibly be better than to be given the instruction manual that teaches you exactly how to please someone? (How many men wish they had one to tell them what women actually want?)

---

[34] Matt 15:24
[35] Isaiah 2:3, Zech 14, etc.
[36] Ex 32
[37] Num 13, 14
[38] Num 25

But despite having that instruction manual, they did not treat God like He was God. Are we guilty of that too? Have we been carefully trained since our youth to think that is a good idea?

## Covenant or Testament?

Not living in a monarchy puts us at a disadvantage as far as understanding loyalty, but living in the western world puts us at an even greater disadvantage because we do not have a cultural understanding as to what a Covenant is.

Covenants are – literally, from ancient times until today, matters of life and death. Purposefully violating the terms of a covenant didn't mean writing a new one or suing someone, it meant that the person had to suffer whatever consequences were listed in the Covenant. Covenants are cumulative; new Covenants never eradicated old ones, but constituted deeper levels of agreement and cooperation between two parties. For example, the Covenant at Sinai did not eradicate God's promise to never destroy the earth again by water, nor did it diminish His Covenant with Abraham to bless the world through his seed. The Covenant of David's kingship also had no lessening effect on the ones that went before it. Deeper relationship brings more intimate levels of Covenant. Think "eternally binding agreement."

Testaments are – man-made legal agreements that can be altered, rewritten, challenged, and often have expiration dates and opt-out clauses. Think "modern contract."

This unfortunate English translation has tragically colored our view of God's eternal expectations, and of His eternal promises. Every day, we see wills being challenged and broken by greedy individuals who want more of what once belonged to someone else. Business agreements are broken if one of the parties to it has a better offer on the table and the funds to deal with potential lawsuits. Marriages are dissolved if the parties just don't "feel the love" anymore. But to the people of what we call the ancient world, Covenants were permanent, even generational, and they were backed by divine authority. Breaking a Covenant between men, based upon blood (personal or by proxy) or salt, was unthinkable and still is in many parts of the world. But we don't understand any of this; we have almost no frame of reference to understand that measure of loyalty and personal integrity – that we will do exactly as we have promised, no matter what – that we would rather die than break our oath. We have lost, culturally, the concept of promises being sacred and forever, and we have sadly foisted our misconception on God as well, as though He is anything like us.

But He isn't – His promises and His idea of forever are extraordinarily different than ours. When He says forever, He doesn't mean until He gets tired of it, or gets angry, or finds something or someone better, or just changes His mind. When He makes a commitment, He will uphold his end forever; we might break His Covenant, but He never will. Throughout the pages of the scriptures we see a recurring theme – that God's reputation is of the utmost importance to Him, and indeed all our hopes rest upon His integrity, trustworthiness and faithfulness.

Ever wonder about Abraham cutting all those animals in half and then falling asleep and watching the flaming torch and smoking oven go between the pieces of the animals?[39] I mean, to modern folks living in the west, it has to be one of the most undecipherable situations in scripture. Why on earth would Abraham cut a bunch of critters in half? It really bothered me, but again, this was something that was so culturally understood even in Jesus' day that no one would even question it.

When two people in ancient times in Mesopotamia (what we now call the "Middle East") would make an irrevocable covenant with each other, they would cut some animals down the middle and then say, "May he who breaks this Covenant have done to him what was done to these animals" as they walked together between the pieces. And they meant it. Nobody was bluffing, this was a matter of generational honor

---

[39] Gen 15

and a man would rather die than fail to live up to the terms of a Covenant ratified in blood. In Jeremiah 34, we see a reference to this type of Covenant

*<sup>18</sup> And I will give the men that have transgressed my covenant, which have not performed the words of the covenant which they had made before me, **when they cut the calf in twain, and passed between the parts thereof,***

*<sup>19</sup> The princes of Judah, and the princes of Jerusalem, the eunuchs, and the priests, **and all the people of the land, which passed between the parts of the calf;***

*<sup>20</sup> I will even give them into the hand of their enemies, and into the hand of them that seek their life: and their dead bodies shall be for meat unto the fowls of the heaven, and to the beasts of the earth.*

But Abraham's Covenant with God was also unique, because of how it would be renewed after his descendants broke it in future generations. Abraham stood there for a long time, waiting for a manifestation of God to come and walk through the pieces with him. Birds came and he had to chase them away, and still he waited. It wasn't until finally Abraham fell supernaturally asleep that the LORD Himself manifested and passed between the pieces in the form of both smoke and fire – just as He would manifest for the children of Israel over 400 years later as they wandered out of Egypt and through the wilderness. By passing through alone, the LORD made a prophetic promise – that when this Covenant would later be broken by Abraham's descendants, the LORD Himself (represented by the smoking furnace) would pay the price on the cross at Calvary so that the eternal Covenant could be renewed in the blood of Jesus. As the original Covenant was between Abraham and God, and because Abraham didn't break the terms of the covenant, God to this day honors that contract with Abraham in that He has promised to never forsake or destroy the *genetic* remnant of Abraham's descendants through Isaac and Jacob.[40]

We all came to the foot of the cross in the first place, knowing we were transgressors of God's perfect, holy, and righteous standard as written in His Torah. We were without excuse – unless His laws were unjust or impossible or unreasonable. Can I get an Amen that we were without excuse?

---

[40] Mal 3:6; Ro 11:26; Jer 31:37, etc.

## What's With the Torch?

Once Abraham fell into the deep sleep, a torch passed between those pieces, as well as the smoking furnace – providing the two witnesses needed to ratify the Covenant. But why a torch?

Each member of the compound unity of God is fully capable of being a witness for the others. In this case, the torch represents the Holy Spirit of God, and this is a really vital thing to know – because when Jesus spoke to His disciples before His arrest, He told them that He was going away but would send another comforter – the Holy Spirit, the Spirit of Truth,[41] the Spirit at work in the Prophets of old. It was the empowering force that gave the Old Testament saints the boldness and authority they needed to do both amazing and everyday things. The Spirit was the seal of God upon their lives.[42] The Jews call this Spirit the Ruach. Yes, the Jews do recognize the Holy Spirit. In fact, you might be shocked to learn how much pre-Messianic literature (Jewish writings before the time of Jesus) has in common with Christian theology, but I digress.

Despite what is often erroneously taught, the Spirit was not first given at Pentecost in Jerusalem. The Spirit was, from the beginning, given whenever it was needed. Look at the account of Exodus 31, where two craftsmen were so full of the Spirit that they could perfectly accomplish all the stone, metal, embroidery, and weaving work of the Tabernacle according to the pattern God showed Moses when he and the 70 elders dined with the LORD Himself![43] Bezaleel and Aholiab had the supernatural ability to get the work done through the Holy Spirit.

Samson had his great strength through the workings of the Spirit. Elijah and Elisha prophesied by the Spirit, as did King David and many others.

---

[41] John 16:13; John 16:7
[42] 2 Cor 1:22, Eph 1:13, 4:30
[43] Ex 24

The Spirit empowers us so that we can do what we are commanded to do.  God would never expect anything from us that we are not capable of – and gives us His Spirit to make sure that it isn't His fault if we don't get the job done.  Just ask Zerubbabel who was undertaking the building of the second Temple after the exile!  How would you like to get a message like this while your enemies are plotting all around you?

*Zech 4:6-9 Then he answered and spoke unto me, saying, This is the word of the LORD unto Zerubbabel, **saying, Not by might, nor by power, but by my Spirit, says the LORD of hosts**. Who art thou, O great mountain? Before Zerubbabel thou shalt become a plain: and he shall bring forth the headstone thereof with shoutings, crying, Grace, grace unto it.  Moreover the word of the LORD came unto me, saying, the hands of Zerubbabel have laid the foundation of this house; his hands shall also finish it; and thou shalt know that the LORD of hosts hath sent me unto you.*

When the Spirit, in the appearance of a torch, passed between the pieces – it was a way of communicating that the divine empowerment and grace needed to get the job of the Covenant done would always be available.  Abraham's covenant keeping offspring would never be abandoned – they would always have help.  Abraham was agreeing that his future descendants would do things God's way, and in exchange, the promised redeemer of the world, prophesied first to Eve in the Garden of Eden, would be born to his lineage.  To secure this promise coming to pass, God was going to have to preserve Abraham's offspring forever.  And we see, despite dreadful persecution at the hands of the world and Christianity, that this promise has been kept.

In the same way as it was given to individuals before Jesus, now we as a Body, since Pentecost, have been given the gift of the Holy Spirit, and have therefore been given what we need to be transformed and to get the work of the Kingdom done.  With God, all things are possible.[44]  Not some things, but *all* things.

And yes, I did say that God has always given His people the grace needed to get the job done.  From Genesis to Revelation, we see grace at work.  Although many theologians have told us that grace was nonexistent before Jesus, the scriptures tell a completely different story because, as I have mentioned before, the LORD does not change.

---

[44] Matt 19:26; Mark 10:27; Phil 4:13

## How God Defines Himself

Whenever God Himself says something, we need to listen intently. When God says something about Himself, it is vitally important that we grasp and accept it as absolute truth.

That's why Exodus 34 is one of my favorite chapters in scripture, because the LORD grants Moses' request to see His glory. Not only does He allow Moses to see as much of it as he can stand, but He also takes the opportunity to define Himself.

*⁵ And the LORD descended in the cloud, and stood with him there, and proclaimed the name of the LORD.*

*⁶ And the LORD passed by before him, and proclaimed, The LORD, The LORD God,* **merciful** *and* **gracious** *,* **longsuffering, and abundant in** **goodness** *and* **truth** *,*

*⁷* **Keeping mercy for thousands,** **forgiving** **iniquity and transgression** **and sin** *, and that will by no means clear the guilty; visiting the iniquity of the fathers upon the children, and upon the children's children, unto the third and to the fourth generation.*

Here on Sinai, after giving the commandments to Moses, the LORD defines Himself as gracious – full of grace. For those of us who were taught that grace first came through Jesus after the resurrection, this is quite the challenge to our thinking. The law would be given, over the course of the next 40 days and nights to Moses on Mt Sinai, and God united the giving of that law with His mercy, His grace and the forgiving nature of His character.[45] He declared Himself as full of grace before giving the law, not 1400 years later.

---

[45] Ex 34:28

Grace, chen in the Hebrew (along with its variants), and charis in the Greek -- is a word meaning mercy, favor, pity, good will, loving kindness. It is one of those words that cannot be adequately related in any single English concept because like all Hebrew words, it embodies both thought and action. Grace is not unmerited favor; it is the embodiment of love in action -- paternal, patient love towards those who are hopelessly flawed (that would be you and me). Unmerited favor is not what a father feels towards His child. Unmerited favor was not what described God's relationship with Noah -- Noah strove for righteousness, a right standing on God's own terms, and that touched our Heavenly Father's heart. I believe that there was something within Noah that cried out "Abba Father," just as with Abraham, Moses, David, and so many others. Despite their flaws, despite the flaws of their children and their children's children, God had mercy on them just as He does with us. God's grace is bound up in His unfailing love. God gives, we reciprocate with our love, devotion and obedience, and He gives more and we reciprocate more in an endless relational cycle.

Grace was available in the times of Noah, at Sinai, and all through what Christians call the Old Testament and Jews call the Tanakh. Jesus didn't bring grace, Jesus was merely the proof that it was always there. The giving of the Holy Spirit, as well, does not mark the arrival of grace but again, is merely a greater manifestation of it, a deepening of the Covenant.

## What's So Holy About the Holy Spirit Anyway?

I never understood what that word meant for a long time – *holy*. I thought it meant "super good." But come to find out, it is the translation of the Hebrew word Qodesh, meaning "set-apart." Set apart -- meaning different, separated, not like everything else, neither common nor defiled. It basically means that something is set aside for a special purpose.

In the Tabernacle and later the Temple, the priests had garments they could never wear outside the boundaries. There were implements – shovels, oil pitchers, special incense, etc. – that could never be used for anything else but serving God. They were only for God, to be used where He wanted and when He wanted and how He wanted, by the specific people He picked out for the job. They were holy.

We are also called to be holy, to be used where He wants, for what He wants, in the way that He wants. When we surrendered our lives to God through the Covenant renewed in Jesus' blood, we were making an agreement with God to live set apart lives, to live His way and not our own way anymore. Whether we knew it or not, we signed an agreement to make Him absolute Master over our lives, both temporal and eternal. We gave Him permission to bless us – and to discipline us. We gave Him permission to adopt us and be our Father. We were not simply signing up for a "get out of hell free" card.

And when we did that, we took within us the Holy Spirit, to teach us all things whatsoever,[46] to instruct us how to live and worship in spirit and in truth.[47] Not just spirit, but spirit and truth. And we must remember that the Holy Spirit of God will never speak in disagreement with the Word of God. In this day and age, it is especially important to search

---

[46] I John 2:27
[47] John 4:24

the scriptures so that we become familiar with what the Spirit will and will not command us to do. If we do not, then we will never be able to discern the difference between our own voice, the voice of the enemy, and the voice of the Spirit. We must always guard ourselves diligently in order to protect ourselves from being deceived. In many ways, we are the most blessed generation who has ever lived – our access to the Bible is unprecedented, our opportunity to read it unparalleled, and our failure to do so tragic. The Holy Spirit will always help us to be conformed into the image of our King, to look more and more like His children daily as we submit to Him in love and trust.

So are we acting like the children of a set apart Creator, or are we acting as though we are the unruly children of an irresponsible father who left his teenagers home while he went away on a long journey, doing as we see fit in the midst of a world who is watching to see if we really are set-apart, or just all talk. They want to see if we hold ourselves to God's standards of what is and is not set apart, clean and unclean, good and bad. They want to know if they do or do not have a reason to honor God based on our behavior.

They want to see if we are really the Children of the Most High, or if Christianity is the biggest hoax in history.

## How Does a Child of the King Behave?

Once we identify ourselves publicly as children of God, eyes are on us for better and for worse. We become subject to judgment – because our Father is unseen and people will largely determine how and what they think of Him based solely upon our actions. He has to ensure that we are faithful witnesses of His standards and His character for the sake of those who are still lost. It is His love for us that holds us to such a high standard. Similarly, in our day to day lives, we also want our own children to represent us well and not make us look bad!

If you are cruel, people will perceive God as cruel.

If you are merciful, people will perceive God as merciful.

If you treat people with justice, they will perceive God as just.

If you play favorites and hold people to differing standards, they will perceive God as a hypocrite.

If you are gracious and patient, they will be willing to trust God.

If you are a nitpicker, they will think God is unpleasable.

If you hold yourself accountable to God's rules, they will see God as the same yesterday, today and tomorrow.

If you live exactly the way you want to, people will not take God seriously at all and will be able to accuse you of picking and choosing according to your liking.

If you live according to the way He says you should live, people will start asking questions – because your behavior is unusual – in a set apart way. If you hold yourself to a higher standard than those around you, people may not agree, but they will start to respect you.

If you don't honor God, neither will they.

We have a severe problem in the Body of Christ – because our behavior really isn't very set apart at all. Some churches emphasize this and others that, because there is no consensus on how we are expected to behave as believers, other than to love each other. And the biggest problem with that is - who gets to have the final say on what love looks like?

On one end, we have a super nice, charitable person who just oozes affection – and on the other end we have clergy seducing the men, women and children in the flock. I submit that in their minds, both of these people might very well classify what they are doing as loving, but if there is no set standard, if no one teaches us exactly what love does and does not look like, then everyone can define it for themselves. If God's standards are subject to our personal opinions, then we are no more able to argue that we are right than anyone else. And if we all believe that we are being led by the Holy Spirit, but our behavior as a body has no continuity, then we definitely need another witness for what we believe the Spirit is telling us. The Holy Spirit would not be telling different people to do different things – He would not tell one person that homosexuality is good and another that it is bad. But right now, that is the image we are projecting to the world, that the "leading of the Holy Spirit" is just a convenient excuse for each person to do whatever they want.

Let's go back to the Father/child picture.

In every family, children are not born to be mature, loving individuals but narcissistic tyrants who, if left to their own devices, will become demanding, horrid adults bent on self-satisfaction.

It is the job of the external influences in a child's life, the family, and especially the parents, to teach a child how to love others. Children do not learn right and wrong on their own, they must be told.  They are not born knowing what is acceptable and unacceptable in how they treat others; they simply respond according to their mood.  If they are angry, they hit and bite, if happy they smile and laugh and hug.  Children are adorable, but until they reach an age where they begin to care about others, their loving actions are largely a matter of trained behaviors and doing whatever feels good at the moment or whatever comes naturally.

In the same way, parents know full well today that we have to teach our children what does and does not constitute what they should receive as love.  For example, we have to teach them that the sexual or physical violation of their bodies is not love, because they just have no framework to defend themselves otherwise.

To sum it up, the child must learn, culturally, what are, and are not, loving actions.  And teaching them is a matter of love, devotion, patience and timing.  It does no good to teach a child calculus before they know addition and subtraction!  But some people go out and expect perfection from immature people right away, which is cruel and unreasonable.  God called us children for a reason; all children need time to grow and learn what is and is not good.

The same goes for all types of behavior.  A baby will stick anything into their mouth once, anything, unless they are warned not to (repeatedly sometimes).  How many of you cringed when I said that, thinking about something horrible your toddler picked up and shoved in their mouth?  One of my sons once brought me a worm with a bite taken out of it.  (I can still hear his sweet little voice, "Wormy dead.") I had to teach him that those were not food!  I laugh about it now, but at the time it was very disconcerting!

Cultures have rules for acceptable and unacceptable apparel, special days – days of mourning and days of rejoicing, what is and is not food, appropriate and inappropriate words and hand gestures – in fact, anyone who has lived in two different countries can relate. Even countries as similar as the United States and Canada have words that mean entirely different things, and you can get into trouble if you don't know what those words are. In fact, when we lived in Canada I once called a little neighbor boy my family's pet name for my little brother. Now as an American, that word was perfectly reasonable, but it happens to be a really profane word there and I got banned from my best friend's house for a long time. So, speaking the same language is not always the same thing as speaking the same language!

It's the same thing when we become children of God; His culture is different than ours, and our lives have to change. Like Ruth, from the Old Testament.

## Ruth and the Culture Shock

I love Ruth so much.  The Book of Ruth is recognized as Messianic prophecy by both Christians and the ancient Jewish sages.  By Messianic prophecy, I mean the entire book points to the character and mission of the Messiah of Israel, even though most of the book is written about a woman – a woman who is in the process of becoming a suitable bride.  It really is a Gospel, because it is literally a story about redemption.

Ruth was a Moabitess,[48] a citizen of one of the two nations of incredibly wicked people descended from the incestuous relationship between Lot and his daughters in the aftermath of the destruction of the cities of the plains, including Sodom and Gomorrah.[49]

When you read about people "making their children pass through the fire,"[50] well, those were Ruth's people!  Chemosh[51] was one of their gods, and his image was a giant, sitting man with the head of a bull with his hands outstretched in front of him.  They would fill the belly of the iron god with fire until he glowed and then the Moabites would take their first born infants and place them into the arms of this evil abomination and watch while they burned to death.  To Ruth growing up, this was normal – and we can only imagine what other evil things they did.  She grew up among people who were incredibly vile – and she is a picture of each one of us, raised in an evil world where a great many first borns are slaughtered legally.

Ruth married the son of the Israelite Naomi and her husband while they were sojourning in Moab during a famine.  Naomi's husband died and then so did both of her sons, leaving Naomi and Ruth and another Moabitess named Orpah as widows.  Naomi told the girls that they were

---

[48] Ruth 1:4
[49] Gen 19:36-37
[50] Deut 18:10
[51] Num 21:29

still young and urged them to return to their fathers because she was going back home to Israel. Orpah left, but Ruth would not and she spoke an incredible Messianic prophecy about our days, one about you and me.

*Ruth 1:16b "Thy people shall be my people, and thy God, my God."*

Ruth was a Gentile, and all she knew about the one true God was whatever she had learned through living with Naomi and her family. That made one thing perfectly clear to her – she did not want to go back to her people and her gods. Something about Naomi's family was different, set-apart, and even though times in Israel were difficult due to the Land recovering from a famine, she would rather go and live with Naomi's people than enjoy the plenty of her own homeland.

I wonder. Was it a legalistic life of bondage that attracted Ruth, or did she perceive that where she was headed was going to be freedom from the way of life she had always known? Maybe Ruth, steeped in a disgusting culture, looked upon the way of life of her mother in law as something worth giving up everything for. Or maybe she saw that she wasn't giving up anything worth having in the first place! In any event, she left the life of her youth and became a part of a foreign culture. Her virtue attracted the attention of a wealthy man who redeemed her, and she became an ancestor of both King David and the promised Messiah.[52] Interestingly, it was her knowledge of the laws of gleaning, land redemption and levirate marriage, and her obedience to them, that brought forth the line of Messiah. Ruth did not live as a Moabitess in Israel, but as an Israelite.

I submit that Ruth was seeking the righteous life that had been modeled for her, not the kind of legalism that required young couples to sacrifice their first born child in the most unthinkably brutal of ways.

---

[52] Matthew 1:5

## What Exactly is Legalism?

I grew up with the mindset that following the "laws of the Jews" was legalism – and yet that was the very life that Ruth chose. So I wanted to know why choosing "legalism" was so pleasing to God that He set this woman in the most important lineage of mankind.

Legalism - strict, literal, or excessive conformity to the law or to a religious or moral code <the institutionalized *legalism* that restricts free choice>[53]

One of the things that shocked me while studying the Bible one day, was the realization that I could never remember seeing the word legalism ever mentioned. In fact, a lot of the words we use in Christianity are never once found in the Bible! Many words, phrases and doctrines are based either on assumptions or are drawn from the writings of famous theologians or personalities over the centuries – and this is one of them.

Premise: Legalistic observance of the "Laws of the Jews" is sin and represents a lack of faith.

Question 1: Can a God with the character we have been laying the foundation for, one who is in unity with Jesus in everything, possibly tell people to sin?

Question 2: Does the concept of "the laws of the Jews" have any merit biblically?

Question 3: Can we find any teaching in the Old Testament (Tanakh) that tells us to observe the letter, without the spirit, of the law.

---

[53] http://www.merriam-webster.com/dictionary/legalism

Answer to Question #1 – No, no, no – God would never command us to sin, not ever – not if the things that Jesus said about Him are true. I believe Jesus, it's always my fallback position on everything and the very premise of this book. Trust Jesus first, trust everyone He tells me to trust, and then interpret everything else based on that foundation. No one else died for me, so I am comfortable with Him being the cornerstone of everything I believe.

Answer to Question #2 – No, it actually doesn't. But then, it does, just not in the context of the Old Testament (Tanakh). We will see that by the time Jesus was born, the laws of the Jews were in full effect – they are referred to as "the traditions of the elders" and they are not found in scripture. The laws given to Moses were given by the mouth of the LORD Himself. Start in Exodus and go straight on through to Deuteronomy and count how many times it says, "And the LORD told Moses, "Speak to the children of Israel and tell them this…"" You might be as shocked as I was to find out that Moses wasn't making this stuff up, that the laws given weren't given by Moses, but through Moses. And can we trust Moses? What did Jesus say?

John 5:46-47 "If you believed Moses, you would have believed Me, for He wrote about Me. But if ye believe not his writings, how shall ye believe my words?"

So right now, I don't know about you, but I am reading clearly that Moses is to be believed, because otherwise Jesus would not have used him for a witness; Jesus wouldn't need to use a legalistic, lying tyrant for a witness. Moses said the laws came from the mouth of God, and who would know that better than the One in unity with God the Father, Jesus!

Answer to Question #3 – No, we can't. Sometimes, it looks as though that is the case, because our translation into English is not always the best, but a deep study of any commandment, especially when taking

60

into account the writings of the prophets, historical context, and the teachings of Jesus, show that the spirit of the law was always supposed to be kept. Jesus said, and the rabbis questioning Him were in full agreement,[54] that the highest laws of all were Deut 6:5 and Lev 19:18. All other laws were to be followed according to the principles of these two; love God with all your heart, mind and being, and love your neighbor as yourself. When the other laws are viewed through those divine filters, the Spirit will guide our judgment – it has always been the case. In everything, we are to act in accordance with the Spirit and the Truth – never sacrificing one for the other or we will be unbalanced. Spirit without truth cannot be the counsel of the Holy Spirit, and truth without the accompaniment of the Holy Spirit is an impossible situation, for the Holy Spirit will always be a witness to truth. This is why Jesus said that upon the royal commandments of loving God and loving our neighbors hang all the other laws.[55]

---

[54] Mark 12:28-34
[55] Matt 22:40

## What is Going on With All These Laws Then?

Can you imagine going through life incredibly nearsighted but not knowing it?

Our Heavenly Father showed me something one morning as I was praying, a way to explain sin because most people have been trained to misunderstand what it is. We were taught to think of sin as intentionally doing something wrong – which has completely warped our thinking, because now to be really considered bad, sin has to have a malicious or lustful sort of quality to it. But that isn't what sin is. There are different Hebrew words for sin, and some of those words clearly delineate intentional vs unintentional vs full blown, spit in God's face rebellion, but sin is basically missing the mark whether one intends to or not, and this is why all have sinned and fallen short of the glory of God.[56]

Imagine target practice without ever having worn a pair of glasses, or even knowing that you needed them. To you, blurry vision is the norm. You have no idea that some people can see clearly. In fact, when people tell you about getting glasses you laugh at them, thinking that you see perfectly already. But then imagine that someone slips a pair of glasses on you while you are sleeping and you wake up with 20/20 vision – just think of going back to the range and seeing where your arrows had actually landed, far from the mark. You'd be embarrassed, because you never saw the target clearly, even though you would have happily sworn on a stack of Bibles that you did. And you'd wish that you'd gotten glasses a long time ago. In fact, you'll probably spend the rest of your life on the target range yelling at people to get glasses, maybe sounding something like Charlton Heston warning people about

---

[56] Ro 3:23

Soylent Green.[57]

In his letters, Paul understands this and tries to explain it – but Paul being Paul, he just never puts anything in plain English (joke intended). Romans 7 is one of those chapters that is hard to understand, because he is never content to just spell things out simply for all us normal folks (I will prove this through Peter's writings in a bit).

I am going to take a small portion of Romans 7:7 and expound upon it as I was shown.

*"Is the law sin? God forbid. Nay, I had not known sin, but by the law"*

Paul says right here that without the law, we do not know what sin is – and no I am not taking it out of context. John agrees.

*I John 3:4 Whosoever committeth sin transgresseth also the law: for sin is the transgression of the law.*

In the church, we were taught to see "the law" as an enemy, but Paul and John both tell us that without it, we cannot clearly see what sin is. And isn't that what we are trying to avoid – sinning? Grace, God's patient, fatherly mercy, has never given us license to sin, not ever, any more than our patient, loving mercy gives our children permission for disobedience.

*Romans 6:15 What then? Shall we sin, because we are not under the law, but under grace? God forbid.*

---

[57]SPOILER ALERT - in case you don't know, Soylent Green was a food that was being fed to the people that was made of – well, people – in the movie of the same name

How do we avoid sinning? What do we have to know in order to define and avoid sin? Paul and John are in agreement – it is the law. The law is not our enemy, but a teacher of God's expectations for a holy and righteous life. Not a self-righteous life, where we come up with our own standards and force them on others, but a righteous life according to His standards. It is the instruction book of a loving Father, and not the dictates of an unreasonable tyrant. Why do the law and the prophets hang from the commandments of Deut 6:5 "Love God" and Lev 19:18 "Love your neighbor?" Because they define how to do those things. To hang from something, there needs to be an attachment – not a separation. Pick the commandments off those two and you are left with absolutely nothing -- no way to love God or our neighbors. No way to avoid sin.

Remember God as Father? The Torah, meaning "instructions," are the rules of His culture, found in the first five books of the Bible. They tell us how to be pleasing to Him, just as any parent teaches their child how to be pleasing. The instructions tell us how to behave ourselves, what is and is not healthy to put into our bodies, how He wants us to dress, how to avoid illness, how to treat the property and lives of others, how to treat our employees and those who owe us money, and how to celebrate with Him and spend time with Him, and how to repent when we have done wrong.

If the rules are there to **convict** us before we accept the blood of Jesus, we need to look at them as instructions to **guide** us after we accept the blood of Jesus. I know this may be hard to accept, because it goes against church doctrines, but does it go against the Bible?

And what exactly and who exactly should be our final authority?

## But What About Paul?

Time and time again, we come across doctrines that are solely based upon the writings of Paul. Don't get me wrong, I love Paul as my brother, but I always remind myself that Paul didn't die for me, and when Jesus was telling His followers who to believe, it was Moses. So now my order of filtering the rest of the Bible is first God/Jesus and then Moses. I have to reconcile everything with their words and if Paul seems to be saying the opposite, I start questioning my understanding of Paul, and not, as I was taught, my understanding of God the Father, Jesus and Moses. There are things we were not taught in Church about Paul – although to be fair, Peter tried to warn us.

*2 Peter 3:15-16 And account that the longsuffering of our Lord is salvation; even as our beloved brother Paul also according to the wisdom given unto him hath written unto you;*

*As also in all his epistles, speaking in them of these things; in **which are some things hard to be understood**, which they that are unlearned and unstable wrest, as they do also the other scriptures, unto their own destruction.*

Paul led an interesting life – he sat at the feet of Gamaliel, the great Jewish sage, and by his own rights, Paul was also a great Jewish sage. He wrote in a style that we do not find anywhere else in the Bible (except by John in certain chapters), and it really is very difficult to understand and very easy to twist, even when, by modern standards, we are very learned. Peter says here that when Paul is twisted, the rest of the scriptures get twisted too. So before we use Paul as a resource, we not only need to understand the Old Testament scriptures fully (as they were the only Bible he or Jesus possessed), but we need to know culturally what Paul knew – some letters he was writing to Jews, and others to former Gentiles – and there are hints in the epistles if one knows what to look for. But assumption and an ill-knowledge of first century history has really kept us at a disadvantage. Paul writes as a first century Jew. He was well versed in the laws of God and the laws of the Jews, he expertly writes in allusions and metaphor, he takes this and that from the scripture and links them together in a markedly rabbinical way, not in a Christian way. He uses Hebraic rules of interpretation to open up the scriptures in order to show that Jesus is the Messiah – and unfortunately, he isn't usually very clear about it. Add the fact that ancient Greek had no punctuation, and only one word for law (when many types of laws are referred to) – well, it really doesn't assist him in being crystal clear to us, let alone his own contemporaries.

When I read Peter's warning about Paul, I laugh a bit. That letter is a clear cut case of damage control. I read it this way,

"And look and see that the longsuffering mercy of our Lord is so that we can be saved; and this is exactly what our beloved brother Paul is trying to say, according to how brilliant and educated he is, when he writes to you. But these letters, when he speaks of these things, are really hard to understand, and so unless you really know what Paul knows and your mind operates the way his does, you are going to grab ahold of them and misinterpret the entire scriptures, and then you'll be in big trouble."

Peter wasn't getting revenge for Paul calling him out for not eating in the homes of the former Gentiles back in Galatia, because he of all people knew he was wrong. This was Peter telling people not to just take Paul's letters at face value, or to solely rely on Paul. And the biggest reason for that? Paul almost never clearly spelled out anything. One verse seems to say this and another verse seems to say entirely the opposite, and yet in all things he refers to Jesus as Messiah, even when he *seems to be* in disagreement with Jesus' teachings. Can that possibly be the case? Peter is backing Paul completely. However, he is saying that anyone who interprets the scriptures through a shallow level reading of Paul is going to be headed to destruction.

A lot of people like to toss out Paul completely, or call him a false apostle, but I have seen many of those people also go on to deny Jesus as Messiah – why? Because without Paul, we do not get the teachings about how maturity brings the fruit of the Spirit, and without the fruit of the Spirit there is no true growth, and people's love for Messiah and one another grows cold.  In addition, once we throw out Paul, we have to throw out 2 Peter, and we have to throw out the book of Acts, written by Luke, and then that means we also have to throw out the Gospel of Luke and I am just not prepared to do that!

So let's start at the Cornerstone, and then go to Moses, and then see how our view of Paul changes.  I submit that he is neither a false apostle nor a false brother.  Let's look at what the Word says, and more importantly, what the Word says about the Word.  The primary law of Biblical interpretation is that we don't interpret the Bible -- the Bible interprets itself.

## What Did Jesus Say About the Law?

Nothing can be more important than what Jesus says about something. Some of the ancient sages of Judaism claimed that all of Creation was made for Messiah, and by Messiah! Therefore, He will be the ultimate source of truth. His words, like Himself, will be eternal. Can I get an amen to that? Can we agree that He would never lie to or mislead anyone? Sometimes (like all rabbis of that day and age) He taught in parables that were confusing or metaphorical, but He never lied or said anything He did not mean.

In fact, can we agree that He never once broke the law in any way? After all, the Bible clearly says that it is a sin to break the law.[58] James said that even breaking one small part is the same as breaking the whole thing,[59] and Jesus was without sin, which means that He never, ever broke the law.[60] Peter also said that Jesus committed no sin.[61] Might I add that James was His own brother – and if Jesus had ever sinned, James would certainly know about it, right? I would certainly be more than happy to spill the beans if either of my two brothers claimed to have led a sinless life.

But then why was He accused of it so often? The Gospels all record some of the Pharisees and scribes accusing him of breaking this or that law – most notably the Sabbath laws.[62] As I mentioned before, the Pharisees (as well as the Essenes, an ultra-orthodox denomination of religious Judaism) had taken it upon themselves to enact thousands of extra-biblical rulings, regarding everything from how to put on one's sandals to the intricacies of what constituted Sabbath observance. And there were different factions that sometimes violently disagreed with

---

[58] I John 3:4
[59] James 2:10
[60] Heb 4:15
[61] I Peter 2:22
[62] Matt 12:10, Mark 3:2, John 9:14-16, Luke 6:2

each other! Some (not all) of these laws were so incredibly oppressive that Jesus said,

*Matthew 23:4 For they bind heavy burdens and grievous to be borne, and lay them on men's shoulders; but they themselves will not move them with one of their fingers.*

These burdens were laid on the Jews by men, not by God and not by Moses – or Jesus would have made it clear. He even makes it plain that if they wished, they could remove those burdens. Why? It is because the rulings were instituted by men and therefore not divinely binding. Sabbath, which was meant to be a delight, had become a burden – so much so that instead of being permitted to fulfill the commandment to love one's neighbor, one ran the risk of whatever they did being labelled as forbidden! Now, that is not to say that the religious leaders were without mercy, for many of their great sages admitted that it was permissible to do good on the Sabbath, and that it fulfilled the law of loving one's neighbor to pull his animal out of a ditch or heal someone – but like all man-made religious rules, nothing can stop men from using them to make accusations against their enemies. In the eyes of some of the Pharisees and scribes, Jesus was a lawbreaker and they were so bent on proving it that they went against even the opinions of some of their own elders in order to do it. They were keeping to the letter, and often ignoring the spirit of the law. They were taking this or that law out of context, and sometimes ignoring all the rest of the Scriptures in order to do so.

Jesus came and taught the law in context, which stripped them of their so-called unlimited divine authority to enforce new regulations to burden the people with. Jesus never, I might add, told them that they didn't have the right to live by those laws if they chose – but when they taught them as being equal to or greater than the laws of God, they were violating the whole of Torah, making the laws of God void, in a matter of speaking – taking away their intended effect of guiding people away from sin by clearly defining it.

*Matt 15:9 But in vain they do worship me, teaching for doctrines the commandments of men.* (Quoting Isaiah 29:13)

*Mark 7:13 Making the word of God of none effect through your tradition, which ye have delivered: and many such like things do ye.*

The Torah was not meant to be a heavy burden, as we will hear from Moses in the next chapter, but the religious leaders made it so incredibly burdensome that the Sabbath was no longer the joyful day of rest intended from the beginning. The entire point of the Law was to set people free and set them apart from the rest of the world, not place them into hopeless bondage.[63] I pointed out that at Mt Sinai, the people who had been in slavery were now free, free to keep the perfect law of liberty, free to be in Covenant with the Creator of the universe. Compared to the way the rest of the world lived, subject to the tyranny of men, false gods and their unjust laws, it is easy to see why the Torah is called the perfect law of liberty. Torah was given for a purpose, and that purpose was for our good and not evil.

What did Jesus say about the nature of the Law of God and His role?

*Matt 5:17-19 **Think not that I am come to destroy the law**, or the prophets: I am not come to destroy, but to **fulfill***. For verily I say unto you, till heaven and earth pass, one jot or one tittle shall in no wise pass from the law, till all be **fulfilled****. Whosoever therefore shall break one of these least commandments, and shall teach men so, he shall be called the least in the kingdom of heaven: but **whosoever shall do and teach them, the same shall be called great in the kingdom of heaven.***

---

[63] James 1:25

I love these verses, but we have an unfortunate translation of two entirely different words as "fulfill." The first is pleroo* and the second is ginomai** – and they don't even sound alike!

Sometimes it is helpful to see where the same words are used elsewhere, to help scripture interpret itself. Let's look at Romans 15:19 – where pleroo is translated as "fully preached." Elsewhere it is translated in such a way as to mean "filled up." What it never means is "done away with." I once heard someone teach, "If my wife is feeling fulfilled, is she feeling filled up with satisfaction or done away with?"

Ginomai is the word that means "come to pass" – far more closely resembling the English meaning of "fulfill" but still not meaning "done away with."

And in context, what did Jesus do after these verses? He starts to "fully preach" a number of commandments, giving them greater integrity, matching up thoughts with outer actions.[64] At no point does He intimate that the law will ever be done away with **until heaven and earth pass** (which does not happen until Rev 21:1, after the 1000 year Millennial reign of Messiah on earth). To drive this point home, He makes some proclamations about who will and will not be great in the Kingdom of Heaven – those who will be great will teach and do the commandments and those who will be least, will break them, and teach others to do the same. Note that this is all in the future and not the present tense. He is not saying, "This holds until I die, then you can do what you want." This is a legally binding statement of the future. Those who teach that there are now only two commandments (Deut 6:5 and Lev 19:18) at this point run into trouble, because one of the commandments clearly states that anyone, ANYONE who adds to or subtracts from the laws given by God through Moses, is by definition, a lawbreaker and a sinner.[65]

---

[64] Matt 5:21-42
[65] Deut 4:2, 12:32

If Jesus told anyone, ever, to break a law or broke a law Himself, then we are still dead in our sins, His sacrifice made invalid. It is impossible for Jesus to have done away with anything in the Torah or the Prophets. It would have invalidated His Messiahship – it would mean He is not One with the Father.

John, James, Peter and the writer of Hebrews make it crystal clear that Jesus is the Messiah of Israel – therefore He could not have done away with any part of the Law. If He did so at the cross, it would mean that He spoke Matt 5:17-18 knowing that it was a lie, and therefore is not Messiah.

We have now established by just a few examples that Jesus kept and upheld the law as eternal before His death. What did He say in His revelation to John?

First of all, He revealed to John that the Serpent was angry only at a certain group of people:

*Rev 12:17 And the dragon was wroth with the woman, and went to make war with the **remnant** of her seed, **which keep the commandments of God, and have the testimony of Jesus Christ**.*

Who is the woman? Israel. Who is the seed? Messiah. Who is the remnant of Israel's Messiah (her seed)? *Those who keep the commandments of God AND have the testimony of Jesus Christ.*

I know it is commonly taught in some Protestant circles that these are two different groups, a first group that keeps the commandments of God, and another group that has the testimony of Jesus Christ. However, if there were two groups, it would have read like this "Those who keep the commandments of God, as well as those who have the testimony of Jesus Christ" – but as you can see there is only one group. Not Jews and Christians, but something in the middle between the two. Jews keep the commandments, and most (not all) deny Jesus, and Christians have the testimony of Jesus but have been carefully trained to not keep the commandments (even though they keep more than they think).

*Rev 14:12 Here is the patience of the **saints**: here are they that **keep the commandments of God, and the faith of Jesus.***

Here, Jesus clearly reveals to John the identity of the saints – they are those who keep the commandments of God and the faith of Jesus as Messiah. Again, this is clearly one group and not two.

*Rev 22:14 **Blessed are they that do his commandments**, that they may have right to the tree of life, and may enter in through the gates into the city.*

Again, Jesus tells us who is allowed to eat from the Tree of Life and enter into the gates of New Jerusalem – they that DO the commandments. Needless to say, by Rev 22 everyone believes that Jesus is Messiah because He has been reigning on earth for 1000 years!

So now, Jesus has established, before His death and even at the end of the age that the commandments are still to be kept by those who are called saints.

Side bar: But I thought there were only two commandments! Or is that one?

## But I Thought There Were Only Two Commandments? Or Maybe One?

*Matt 22:36-40 Master, which is the great commandment in the law? Jesus said unto him, Thou shalt love the Lord thy God with all thy heart, and with all thy soul, and with all thy mind. This is the first and great commandment. And the second is like unto it, Thou shalt love thy neighbour as thyself.* **On these two commandments hang all the law and the prophets.**

*John 13:34 A* **new commandment** *I give unto you, that ye love one another; as I have loved you, that ye also love one another.*

Christian theologians will often say that one of these two scenarios applies.  Either (1) there are only two commandments now – love God and love your neighbor (by their definition of what love looks like) or (2) there is only one commandment now, "love one another."

If Jesus whittled down the laws of the Father to only two commandments, He would have broken Deut 4:2 and 12:32, which clearly command us not to add or subtract.  At this point, as I have said before, the Pharisees and Scribes would have had legal grounds to have Him executed as a false prophet under the guidelines set up in Deut 13 – in fact, everything they did to Him was an attempt to see whether or not they could disqualify Him as the Messiah, the prophet of whom Moses prophesied.

*Deut 13:1-5* **If there arise among you a prophet**, *or a dreamer of dreams, and* **giveth thee a sign or a wonder** (definitely applied to Jesus) *And the sign or the wonder come to pass, whereof he spake unto thee,* **saying, Let us go after other gods, which thou hast not known, and let us serve them**; (by declaring new laws or destroying existing ones, Jesus would have been preaching another god, whom they had not known)

**Thou shalt not hearken unto the words of that prophet**, *or that dreamer of dreams:* **for the LORD your God proveth you, to know whether ye love the LORD your God with all your heart and with all**

*your soul.* (God gave fair warning that false prophets and teachers are there to test our devotion)

*Ye shall walk after the LORD your God, and fear him, and keep his commandments, and obey his voice, and ye shall serve him, and cleave unto him*. (This is how we were instructed to protect ourselves from following after false prophets, by knowing and keeping God's commandments and only God's commandments)

*And that prophet, or that dreamer of dreams, shall be put to death; because he hath spoken to turn you away from the LORD your God, which brought you out of the land of Egypt, and redeemed you out of the house of bondage, to thrust thee out of the way which the LORD thy God commanded thee to walk in. So shalt thou put the evil away from the midst of thee.*

(This was the heart of the matter, Jesus was challenging their authority, and their laws, and so in order to accuse Him successfully and kill Him, they had to get Him to change the laws as given to Moses. They then would have had the legal right under God's Laws to put Him to death, which they were never able to do until he claimed he was the LORD at His illegal trial. At that point *in their opinion* they had Him for blasphemy.)

As an aside, there are many folks who bitterly hate those who tested Jesus, but we have to look at what was going on from the standpoint of what they were required to do biblically in order to test anyone claiming to be the prophet of whom Moses spoke. Jesus was doing miracles. He claimed to be Messiah. It was their obligation to test Him in order to not fall prey to a false prophet or false Messiah, as it was written. Yes, some of the religious leaders were testing Him unrighteously, but I believe that a great many were testing him righteously and wisely. We cannot paint any group of people with the same wide brush, as there were Pharisees and Scribes who were deeply and truly devoted to God, just as there are today. They, just like us, have an obligation to test everything. A denomination cannot be judged for the actions of a few leaders - especially when that denomination is as diverse as the first century Pharisees.

Back to the point in question, what Jesus did was to simply tell them what they already knew. He gave them the spiritual filters through which the entire law and prophets were to be administrated. Love God with everything you have, and love your neighbor as yourself. These were not strange commandments – they were already part of the Torah law – Deut 6:5 and Lev 19:18, but they can be seen in every single commandment, when viewed through Hebraic glasses. There was nothing new here, and the Pharisees and scribes in attendance admitted that He was absolutely correct.[66]

What about the verse in John narrowing everything down to one "new" commandment? First of all, let's look at the word "new" in Greek.

Greek has two words for new – the first is neos, which means brand new – like you got a neos pair of shoes because the old ones fell apart. The second is kainos, which means "renewed" like the moon every month. When the moon goes black and the sky is darkened, it looks like the moon disappears and then with the first sliver sighting a day or two later, we get a new moon – but it isn't a neos moon, it is a kainos moon. It is simply renewed, and we can see the moon again.

So for Jesus to say we have a *neos* command, again, He would have broken the Law of God, and would have been counted as a transgressor and we would be dead in our sins, separated from the Covenants of promise. But Jesus instead said that we have a *kainos* command, thereby making something visible again which had been clouded or obscured – in this case, by many years of religious traditions that created strife and animosity between those seeking God, both Jew and Gentile. I will cover this in my chapter about Peter and his Acts 10 vision.

---

[66] Mark 12:28-34

What Jesus did here is no different than when we tell our kids, on the way to Grandma's house, "Now behave yourselves!" We have narrowed all of our commandments down to a single concept. Our kids know darned well that "Behave yourself!" means no fighting, or breaking anything, or swearing, or being disrespectful or disobedient. When the law is summarized into two commandments, it is the same thing as when we summarize everything we have ever taught our kids into a single "reminder phrase." Again, we see that God operates by Father/child principles, just like we do.

That doesn't stop our kids from getting rowdy and breaking something at Grandma's house and saying, "You only said to behave ourselves, you didn't say we couldn't roughhouse!"

But we all know that they knew, just like we knew when we were kids – our commandments were not that difficult! Unless Grandma loaded us up with sugar, then they got really difficult!

Now, these commandments of our Heavenly Father – are they too difficult? Does the Bible say anywhere that the laws handed down by the LORD to Moses are too difficult?

## What Did Moses Say About the Law?

By Jesus' own words, we have established Moses as an honest witness. So really, that cinches his resume for me. That's the ultimate character reference, when Messiah says, "If you believed Him, you would believe me, because He wrote about me!" Every author would like that kind of recommendation on their dust jacket.

So anything we have handed down from Moses is a faithful witness – if it were not, then Jesus would certainly have pointed it out. Moses' writings are therefore above reproach.

One of the last things Moses said before his death was this, after retelling the commandments to the entire Nation of Israel --

*Deut 30:11-16 For this commandment which I command thee this day, it is not hidden from thee, neither is it far off. It is not in heaven, that thou shouldest say, Who shall go up for us to heaven, and bring it unto us, that we may hear it, and do it? Neither is it beyond the sea, that thou shouldest say, who shall go over the sea for us, and bring it unto us, that we may hear it, and do it? But the word is very nigh unto thee, in thy mouth, and in thy heart, that **thou mayest do it**. See, I have set before thee this day life and good, and death and evil; in that **I command thee this day to love the LORD thy God, to walk in his ways, and to keep his commandments and his statutes and his judgments, that thou mayest live** and multiply: and **the LORD thy God shall bless thee** in the land whither thou goest to possess it.*

Moses never said, "Well, hopefully you might be able to do the commandments." He said, "You can do them. It isn't hidden, or too far out of your reach, but in your mouth and in your heart." It also says something we will discuss later on – that we love God *by* keeping His commandments, and statutes, and judgments. Perhaps you remember

Jesus saying that as well – "If you love me, keep my commandments."[67] Remember that Jesus said Moses wrote about Him? Loving the LORD, from the beginning, has always been tied together with trusting and respecting Him enough to obey His commandments. When we visibly obey God in the sight of the world, we honor Him (increase His good reputation), just as our children honor us by behaving according to our standards in public.

What else did Moses write?

*Deut 29:14-15 Neither with you only do I make this covenant and this oath; But with him that standeth here with us this day before the LORD our God, **and also with him that is not here with us this day:***

The Covenant was not only made with those present at the time it was given, but with all those who, in the future, would join themselves to serve the God of Abraham, Isaac and Jacob. That's us, and that means that all of God's promises, all of His commandments, belong to us – not as burdensome obligations, but setting us apart as a peculiar people. We aren't like everyone else – we belong to God's eternal family. We aren't second class citizens, nor are we any better than the native born.[68]

There is one law for the native born and the foreigner, the same justice for all.[69]

*Lev 25:18 Wherefore ye shall do my statutes, and keep my judgments, and do them; and ye shall dwell in the land in safety.*

*Deut 13:4 Ye shall walk after the LORD your God, and fear him, and keep his commandments, and obey his voice, and ye shall serve him, and cleave unto him.*

---

[67] John 14:15
[68] Ro 11:18
[69] Ex 12:49; Num 9:14

*Deut 7:9 Know therefore that the LORD thy God, he is God, the faithful God, which keepeth covenant and mercy with them that love him and keep his commandments to a thousand generations;*

These three verses are extremely challenging for anyone who makes the claim that the law is impossible to keep because they are left in the unenviable position of judging God's integrity, as well as Jesus'. Of course, we never thought of it that way, we were simply taught that something was true for so long that we read over these verses without even thinking about it. That's called conditioning, when you are told something so many times that you accept it as fact, so completely that you can read something clearly to the contrary and not even see it. And the people who taught us these things, they were the victims of conditioning too. It doesn't even do any good to get angry about it. Conditioning doesn't mean we were stupid, it just means that we were diligently trained to accept a lie as reality, just like our ancestors!

God says, "You will do my statues, and judge with my judgments, and I will bless you." (Lev 25:18 paraphrase mine)

Moses says, "You will keep His commandments and obey Him and serve Him and cleave to Him." And also, "He is faithful and will keep the Covenant with those who love Him and keep His commandments to a thousand generations." (Deut 13:4 and 7:9 paraphrase mine)

That is an interesting point. A thousand generations. If a generation is even just 20 years, then 1000 times that is 20,000 years – that is how long God will bless those who keep His commandments. Sinai happened roughly 3500 years ago. A thousand generations is a long, long time from now – and certainly did not come to an abrupt halt 2000 years ago, ending the obligation to keep those commandments.

Are there any scriptures to back this up? Is there an expiration date on the commandments?

*Ex 31:16 Wherefore the children of Israel shall keep the sabbath, to observe the sabbath throughout their generations, for a **perpetual covenant.***

*Lev 16:34 And this shall be an **everlasting statute** unto you, to make an atonement for the children of Israel for all their sins once a year. And he did as the LORD commanded Moses.*

*Lev 24:8 Every sabbath he shall set it in order before the LORD continually, being taken from the children of Israel by an **everlasting covenant**.*

*Num 25:13 And he shall have it, and his seed after him, even the covenant of an **everlasting priesthood**; because he was zealous for his God, and made an atonement for the children of Israel.*

May I submit that God knows exactly what the definitions of words like "perpetual," and "everlasting" (or as some versions translate "forever" and "eternal") mean? When God says forever, it isn't like when we say forever – because He is forever! He was, is and always will be! At no point does "forever" cease to exist for Him, even though our limited existence in the flesh makes it hard for us to think in forever terms.

Now, there is a doctrine that is commonly taught in the churches that I want to lay out for your consideration before we look at what Paul had to say about the Law.

The doctrine goes like this – "The law was given to prove that we needed Jesus to save us, because it was impossible to keep."

## Are the Jews the Chosen People or Just Some Cruel Sociological Experiment?

I know that people hate it when I put it in those terms. But sometimes we just have to be blunt because we only have two possible scenarios. Sometimes we have to question what we believe and what that belief really says about our true opinion of the character of our Heavenly Father and His Son (since they are one, what we say about the character of one applies to the other).

#1 – Jesus and Moses and God were right and the laws are good and not impossible to keep, and they are also eternal in nature.

OR

#2 – the Hebrew people were told that they could, and had better, keep a system of impossible requirements, and then were punished and cast aside when they inevitably failed. All this was done just to prove that they needed a Messiah who was not going to show up for a very long time.

I ask you, what is the character of the Father that Jesus preached? Jesus is One with the Father, and so which of these positions can be justified by the revealed character of the Son and the Father?

Would the God we serve do something so incredibly horrible to people, giving them no chance whatsoever to succeed – just to prove a point? Would He repeatedly, through Moses and the prophets, lie to His chosen people, and tell them that they could make this system work? Furthermore, is God even capable of making bad or unreasonable laws, a legalistic system of horrific proportions? What would you think of a human leader who would do such a thing to people? You would think he was a psychopath! Is it even remotely possible that the second scenario is reasonable?

If you still think that doctrine is sound, I am about to blow your mind. What if I told you that there were people in scripture who were called blameless?  Elizabeth and Zechariah, the parents of John the Baptist, walked in all the commandments and ordinances blamelessly.[70]  And the Apostle Paul was also blameless according to the letter of the law.[71]  What about all the New Testament verses saying that we, as well as the leadership within the body, are to be blameless.[72]  If the law was impossible to keep blamelessly, then how did Elizabeth, Zechariah and Paul manage to do it at all?  And how were NT leaders supposed to do it without "falling from grace?"

We are clearly missing something.

Here's the deal – a lot of folks, and I believe a great many people of faith, were raised in homes where the fathers did exactly according to that doctrine.  They set up unreasonable standards, and even when those standards were met, they were still denied approval and recognition.  It is crushing to a child to be told to jump this high, and then work at it until they accomplish it, only to be told that it isn't good enough.  There are verses that talk about this --

*Pro 13:12 Hope deferred maketh the heart sick: but when the desire cometh, it is a tree of life.*

*Col 3:21 Fathers, provoke not your children to anger, lest they be discouraged.*

Children, in order to thrive and become healthy, loving adults, need to be able to have attainable goals.  We need to be able to have our hopes come to fruition. When we are told what to do and we do it, we need to have that be good enough in the eyes of our parents.  When that hope is deferred, endlessly squashed, a child loses hope and may eventually stop trying.  But when that hope is satisfied through parental approval and love, it really is like a tree of life.  Being able to make a parent happy with us – well, it's the deferred dream of many wounded children

---

[70] Luke 1:6

[71] Phil 3:6

[72] I Cor 1:8; I Tim 3:2; etc.

86

and adults. And it wouldn't be in the Bible if God Himself didn't recognize it as true. Tragically, I believe a great many clergymen grew up in such families, especially during the middle ages and Renaissance when the "second sons" of noble families were barely looked at and then passed off into the church to get rid of them. We probably had a great many angry, brokenhearted men in the pulpits preaching their idea of our Heavenly Father based on their very unheavenly fathers, which breaks my heart.

But Jesus said that we have a good Father. Not a Father to withhold praise and blessing when His children are striving to do what He wants them to do, but a Father who is so in love with His children that He gave His own Son to die in order to redeem them and bring them close again. We cannot reconcile a God who would make such an effort to save us, with a God who has given us no way to please Him.

And if He was that kind of God, He certainly would not be pleased with people who still don't do what He says after He made a path for restoration to the Covenant through Jesus.

Either God cares about His laws, or he doesn't.

His laws are either good or bad.

His laws are either detrimental or beneficial.

Let us go to one of the most profound things Moses ever said,

*Deut 10:12-13 And now, Israel, **what doth the LORD thy God require of thee**, but to fear the LORD thy God, **to walk in all his ways**, and to **love him**, and to serve the LORD thy God with all thy heart and with all thy soul, **to keep the commandments of the LORD**, and his statutes, **which I command thee this day for thy good**?*

God requires us to fear/respect Him, love him, serve Him, and to keep His commandments and statutes – which were given for our benefit!

We have already established Moses as the witness Jesus chose, he even spoke face to face with the LORD as a man speaks with his friend.[73] Moses says the commands are for our good – which means that we can no longer logically entertain the notion that they were given simply to prove we couldn't live up to them.  There is certainly nothing good for us in that!  That would simply provoke us to anger and hopelessness.

Jesus reiterated what Moses said, and at the same time, claimed His divinity.

*John 14:15 "If ye love me, keep **my** commandments."*

Make no mistake, there are those who say that Jesus never claimed to be divine, but when He said this, He was making a clear statement that He is one and the same with the LORD Moses spoke of, the One who gave the commandments at Mt Sinai.

---

[73] Ex 33:11

## So What About Paul – Pt 2

A lot of times, we get into a pickle because the only way we can justify believing or doing something (or not doing something) is through quoting Paul, and that is troublesome. It is a matter of Biblical law (of which Paul was an expert) that no matter can be established by less than two separate witnesses.[74] This means, if Paul is the only person who seems to be saying something, it is not established, and no, it doesn't count if he says it twice. Two witnesses = two different people. But the good news is that, as we learn the rest of scriptures and look again at what Paul is saying, we see that he never really disagrees with the rest of scripture – we simply lacked the context. Otherwise, how can we read a verse saying the law is good and another saying the law is bad and choose to believe the verse saying the law is bad – when the verse about the law being good is witnessed over and over again from Genesis through Revelation? And no one else says that the law is bad!

So what law is lacking, because Paul really digs harshly into something called "the law." Can we find another law that is also criticized that would give us another witness? How about two more witnesses?

In my chapter on *What Did Jesus Have to Say About the Law*, I mentioned a few verses, quotes from both Jesus and the prophet Isaiah, which were clearly speaking against a certain kind of law.[75]

That criticized law is called, in scripture, "the traditions of the elders." Even today, when an observant Orthodox Jew speaks of observing Torah, he is actually speaking of observing Torah according to the traditions of the elders. It is an unspoken truth – but they will gladly verify this if you ask them.

---

[74] Deut 17:6, 19:15; Matt 18:16; 2 Cor 13:1; I Tim 5:19
[75] Is 29:13; Matt 15:9; Mark 7:13

What I just pointed out is virtually unknown in Christian circles because it is not widely taught from the pulpit. Perhaps you have heard of the Talmud? The Talmud was compiled from the oral teachings handed down generation after generation by rabbis who claimed that Moses received not one, but two revelations on Mt Sinai, one to be written down and another to be passed along by word of mouth. You can see how problematic this is, because even if it were true (and it is written that Moses wrote all the words that God gave him[76]), people over the 1400 years between Sinai and Jesus' ministry could have added to and subtracted from them – and we see from the very writings of the Talmud (compiled between 200 and 600 AD) that the legal orthodox Jewish requirements have gone through alterations. The Talmud is largely a book of Jewish laws and commentary, in essence, no different than we find in books on Catholicism and Protestant Christianity, except that the writings of the sages have been combined into one large text to be compared side by side so it can easily be seen what many ancient sages said about a given topic or dispute.

The traditions of the elders largely defined what it was to be a religious Jew in Jesus' day, and in some ways, greatly departed from the law given at Mt Sinai. For instance, at Mt Sinai there was no separation between the natural born Hebrews and the foreigners who attached themselves to God, but in Jesus' day, there was a great wall of legal division, not in any way justified by the Torah as given through Moses.

There were many of these extra rulings, and at this point they weren't even written down so no one could hope to keep what they thought was the Torah without spending many, many hours at the feet of the Rabbis who taught them – like Paul did. The common people who kept them were doing the best they could. They had no Bibles in their homes, and so they could not cross-reference what they were being

---

[76] Ex 24:4

told. Questioning religious authority has always been potentially dangerous business, and it was no different back then. Do according to the edicts of the Rabbis, or be judged by them as transgressors, which is exactly what they did to Jesus. It is much the same in Christianity today – there is indeed nothing new under the sun!

And yet Paul never distanced himself from being a Pharisee,[77] and that is very important to realize, even though he spoke against certain practices. What he absolutely distanced himself from were the "works of the law,"[78] a concept very much misunderstood until the finding and study of the Dead Sea Scrolls. Pharisaic Judaism held (and still holds) the sanctity of human life above almost any commandment. This beautiful concept is called Pikuach Nefesh ("saving lives"), and really demonstrates that the "spirit of the law" is an entirely Jewish concept. One notable exception to the concept of being permitted to break a commandment in order to save a life is that one may never commit any sort of idolatry. As the first commandment is to love God first and foremost and then love our neighbor, this does not violate Messiah's teachings, but instead validates them.

However, many of the "works of the law" had absolutely no respect for Pikuach Nefesh whatsoever, and are therefore entirely un-Hebraic in nature. According to the works of the law practiced by the Essenes of Paul's day (an excessively strict and rigid form of Judaism), it was not permissible to break even the smallest law in order to save life. It was better to watch a man die than to lift a finger to help him on the Sabbath. We see from the Dead Sea Scrolls 4QMMT that the members of the Essene community were ranked and judged according to how well they kept the rigid halakah of their sect. It was a merciless form of religious observance that taught justification based upon their system of works. Unfortunately, in Rome and Galatia, its poison found its way into

---

[77] Acts 23:6
[78] Ro 9:32; Gal 2:16; Gal 3:2, 5, 10

the believing community as former Essenes became believers in Jesus as Messiah. Paul fought this incursion of Essene practices tooth and nail. Now, I don't want people getting the wrong idea about the Essenes, because they were also great champions against the corruption that Greece and Rome brought into the Judaism of the day, like the selling of the Aaronic priesthood to the highest bidder. They simply went too far in some areas.

And so one of the important things to understand about Paul is that he is writing about very complex theological situations to the very people who were living in the midst of the controversies. On one hand, we have the Torah as given to Moses, and on the other hand we have the oral Torah (traditions of the elders) of the Pharisees, and on someone else's hand we have the deadly works of the law of the Essenes. Paul was addressing, in letters, people who were living with all these groups and who were well acquainted with these three sometimes conflicting world views.

Paul sat at the feet of the great Rabban Gamaliel, the grandson of Hillel I, and so if anyone knew the written and the oral law and the works of the law it was Paul. If anyone knew the hazards of the first century religious landscape, it was Paul. And so when he criticizes a set of laws – do you think he was agreeing with Jesus and Isaiah? Or do you think he was disagreeing with them?

Paul was an expert on the law of God, remember, and according to his own words in 2 Cor13:1 and I Tim 5:19, he knew the two witness rule. He knew he could not say anything that lacked two witnesses. That means he couldn't criticize something that the Word praises more than once.

## Understanding Paul's Epistles as Letters

I am going to ask you to read a letter out of context just to see what your honest evaluation of the situation is:

Dear Sam,

Well it was great hearing from you again, and I can't wait until we can come visit! Seems like forever since we were in Liverpool, and the chips we had at that place downtown were just THE BEST!

I was so shocked to hear about Charlie in prison! But then, not really much of a surprise once I thought about it -- he was always awkward around the kids, wasn't he? Maybe he can get things turned around for the better. Give me his address so I can send him a Bible, will you please? We are praying for him.

As for Violet, I agree that she should not be teaching men like that! Let the men do it. It would be entirely inappropriate for her to be a part of that. Her heart is in the right place, but she would be better off with the women and children.

Best Regards,

Your brother Paul

Now honestly, I want your first impressions
#1 -- what country is Sam from, and what sort of food is Paul referring to?
#2 -- what can you discern of Charlie's character, and his past and present situation?
#3   why doesn't Paul approve of Violet teaching men?

The answer to all three should be -- "I have no idea, there is not enough information given."

Now it would be easier if we had the letter that this was a response to.

Dear Paul,

How are ya'll doing in Chicago? Everyone here in Texas sure misses you -- and Trudy down at the deli says she has a bag of those Takis all put aside for you. She still laughs about how much you loved them, like you'd never seen a Mexican chip before!

You are not going to believe this, but remember Charlie the youth group leader? Well, come to find out, he hated it and was only in it to please his parents. So Greg got him started in prison ministry and he loves it! He has started a Bible drive and everything. I think he is going to make a big difference there!

Here is the issue though, and I want your honest opinion. His sister Violet, well, you know what a heart of gold she has, and I never met anyone so trusting. Well, she wants to go in there teaching right alongside him. I'm against it because she's always falling for some sob story and getting herself into deep trouble. Now, if it were Jackie, her mom, that would be one thing -- that woman is tough as nails, but I think Violet is absolutely the worst possible candidate for men's prison ministry. And this isn't a white collar facility, these are violent felons! She has been offered a chance to teach at the local women's shelter, which I think she would be great at, with her compassion --but for some reason she is always wanting to save guys who end up walking all over her. I know she takes your advice really seriously, so can you please put in a good word? Thanks.

Sam

Now be honest. You probably thought or at least strongly suspected that Sam was from Britain, they were talking about french fries, that Charlie was in jail for child molestation, that the Bible was for his salvation and that Paul was saying women shouldn't teach men at all, and stick to teaching women and children.  And that's because my fictitious Paul had no obligation to write detailed accounts of what questions he was answering because he was writing to the person who asked the questions in the first place.   You filled in the blanks logically with details from your sphere of reference, just like we all naturally are inclined to do.  (And yes there is a Liverpool, Texas)

If that response letter had been taught in church by itself, what sort of doctrine could be built around it?  And just think of poor Charlie's reputation, way worse than Thomas'.

You see, when we do not have all the information, and we teach as though we do -- it is going to amount to presumptuous gossip.  And we have all gossiped about Paul for many years.  Paul believes this, and forbids that, etc.... even when we don't have the other side of the correspondence (and don't even get me going on the fact that neither ancient Greek nor Hebrew had any punctuation!).  I am not saying that it is a bad thing to try to understand Paul's letters, but when we create doctrines using them for others to follow, we are on unstable ground when we are clearly commanded to stand upon the Rock.  Or in biblical terms, we are down in the wadi when we should be up top on the rocky ledge.  There is more than enough sound doctrine to be had in the Old Testament, supported by the teachings of Jesus -- and so unless we can line up a "Pauline" doctrine or understanding solidly with the rest of scripture, then we have to admit that it might just chalk up to nothing more than gossip.

I love and cherish Paul's letters, but they are indeed letters, and one-side of a conversation (did you know what we are missing one of his letters to the Corinthians?[79]) and I won't bet anyone's salvation on my (or anyone else's) ability to interpret them 100% correctly.

We know what they taught us Paul meant, but as I like to tell people, what we actually do will always speak louder than what we say. So what did Paul actually do in real life?

---

[79] I Cor 5:9

## What Does Paul's Life After Salvation Say About the Law?

*Acts 28:7b Men and brethren, though **I have committed nothing against the people, or customs of our fathers**, yet was I delivered prisoner from Jerusalem into the hands of the Romans.*

So, did Paul live like a Gentile after his Damascus road experience? There were certainly accusations of just that spread all over Jerusalem! There were unbelieving Jews, as well as believing Pharisees, who accused him of not living according to the Law as given to Moses. So, let's first look at the accusations, as recorded by Luke, also the writer of the gospel of Luke. There were a lot of accusations spread out over a few chapters, but this one sums it up nicely

*Acts 21:21 And they are informed of thee, that **thou teachest** all the Jews which are among the Gentiles to **forsake Moses**, saying that they ought not to circumcise their children, neither to walk after the customs.*

So, in a nutshell, people were going around saying that Paul was telling people not to follow the Law given through Moses – with specific charges that he was teaching against circumcision. This charge was related to Paul by James, the first leader of the believers in Jesus as Messiah, also the brother of Jesus.

What was James' own response – did James give any credence whatsoever to the charges?

*[23] Do therefore this that we say to thee: We have four men which have a vow on them;*

*[24] Them take, and purify thyself with them, and be at charges with them, that they may shave their heads: and **all may know that those things, whereof they were informed concerning thee, are nothing; but that thou thyself also walkest orderly, and keepest the law.***

Now, if Paul was indeed living apart from the Law, then James would be literally conspiring with him here to deceive people. So now, in order to believe that Paul did not keep the Law, we have to call into question the character not only of Luke who wrote the account, but also of James, the brother of Jesus.

So what did Paul end up doing? Did he say, "No way, anyone who keeps one commandment has to keep them all!" No, this is what he did.

*26 Then Paul took the men, and the next day purifying himself with them entered into the temple, to signify the accomplishment of the days of purification, until that an offering should be offered for every one of them.*

First of all, he was baptized (purified) as the law commands before entering the Temple. In Hebrew, it is called a mikveh, and everywhere in the Torah where you see someone who is ritually unclean having to wash themselves before going to the Tabernacle or Temple, that is what Paul did here. Baptism was nothing new, and is not a uniquely Christian doctrine. Then he entered the Temple and we see that he kept the law of the Nazirite vow[80] that he had been undertaking since at least Acts 18:18, perhaps being at the end of it and purifying himself, as these other believers were beginning their vows. This vow required a sacrifice at the Temple (I know the translation says offering, but the only offering they could have given was a burnt offering, not a monetary offering). All of this was in accordance with the Law given to Moses.

(This is where we need to counter a fallacy of teaching – the overwhelming majority of animal sacrifices in the Law of God had absolutely nothing to do with sin. Jesus took away our need for animal sacrifice for sin, by taking our death penalty for us, not by doing away

---

[80] Num 6

with the requirement.  When we sin, repent, and ask forgiveness, we are pleading that blood offering on our behalf so that we can draw near to God again.  The Hebrew word for sacrifice is korban, which a root meaning of drawing near or approaching  Most Temple sacrifices were for thanksgiving and peace and as gifts or as part of the Feasts, and were for the purpose of honoring God and drawing near.)

So here, we see Paul keeping the laws concerning the Temple.  You will notice that they are not referred to as ceremonial laws (another term that is found nowhere outside of commentary), and if they have been done away with, then James, Paul and these four men are all "falling from grace" instead of proving themselves to be faithful followers of God.

Let us look at another accusation – whether or not Paul was teaching against circumcision.

*Acts 16:3 Him would Paul have to go forth with him; **and took and circumcised him** because of the Jews which were in those quarters: for they knew all that his father was a Greek.*

Paul circumcised Timothy himself.  This one is hard to reconcile with what we have been taught – namely that it was Paul's assertion that anyone who becomes circumcised is cut off from the Covenant.  I will clarify this later in a chapter about circumcision, a word with two entirely different first century meanings.  Needless to say, however, I can assure you that Paul did not sin against Timothy by jeopardizing his salvation.

Here's another example:

*Acts 23:5 Then said Paul, I wist not, brethren, that he was the high priest: for **it is written**, Thou shalt not speak evil of the ruler of thy people.*

Paul had just been busted across the chops by the High Priest. He lost his temper and rebuked his attacker publicly. When it was pointed out that this was the High Priest, Paul repented of his sin, as per the Torah of the LORD.[81] Regardless of whether or not we feel the High Priest had it coming, Paul kept the commandment of God.

*Acts 24:14 But this I confess unto thee, that after the way which they call heresy, so **worship I the God of my fathers, believing all things which are written in the law and in the prophets:***

Here Paul defends himself by saying he believes all things which are written in the law and the prophets. The law and the prophets say that the law is eternal, forever, everlasting. The law and the prophets say that we can and must keep the commandments.

So, by Paul's own testimony related through Luke, if Paul seems to say anything that contradicts the law and the prophets – then we are simply misunderstanding him. Paul had one of the greatest legal minds in history, a mind like a steel trap, and I think we haven't been taught to give him enough credit for being able to write at seriously deep and, to us, confusing levels. Peter knew, Peter warned us.

But Peter also cherished Paul – because Paul saw the depths of the relationship we should have with our God in so many amazing ways. One of the most wonderful ways was according to the Master/bondservant relationship – but unfortunately, in the Americas and Europe, our ideas about servants and slaves have been dreadfully

---

[81] Ex 22:28

contaminated by an abominable form of slavery that is Biblically indefensible – even though the Bible was blasphemously used to support it.

## Bondservant or Freeman?

Romans Chapter 1 starts out like this –

*Paul, a servant of Jesus Christ, called to be an apostle, separated unto the gospel of God,*

In making this proclamation, Paul[82] wasn't talking about what we brutally think of when we read the word duolos, meaning slave, but was referring back to Exodus 21 – something that every believer of the time would have understood. In ancient Israel, it was the law that when an Israelite could not pay off his debts, that he would sell himself into slavery as an honorable way to settle his debts. But the sale was only for 6 years of service, after which time he was a free man. Not so long ago in Europe and America, we called something very similar to it indentured servitude.

*¹ Now these are the judgments which thou shalt set before them.*

*² If thou buy an Hebrew servant, six years he shall serve: and in the seventh he shall go out free for nothing.*

*³ If he came in by himself, he shall go out by himself: if he were married, then his wife shall go out with him.*

*⁴ If his master have given him a wife, and she have born him sons or daughters; the wife and her children shall be her master's, and he shall go out by himself.*

***⁵ And if the servant shall plainly say, I love my master, my wife, and my children; I will not go out free:***

---

[82] In addition, Paul repeated this in Titus 1:1; Peter in II Peter 1:1, James in James 1:1, Jude in Jude 1, and John in Rev 1:1

*⁶ Then his master shall bring him unto the judges; he shall also bring him to the door, or unto the door post; and his master shall bore his ear through with an aul; and he shall serve him for ever.*

When Paul declared himself to be a bondservant, he was stating that he had been in debt to sin, that his debt had been bought off by his Master Jesus and that he never wanted to leave Him, but instead desired to serve Him forever.

Bondservants were not like the slaves we think of – they were trusted by their masters and given authority to buy and sell and do business in the name of their masters. And this was exactly the sort of "slave" or duolos that Paul was. Think of Abraham's servant, from Genesis 24, who was sent hundreds of miles with camels laden with precious things to find a bride for Isaac – this was not a slave who might run away, this was a trusted member of the family.

In the same way, Paul was sent hundreds of miles by his Master in order to go searching for a Bride. Slaves do not serve out of love, but under compulsion – bondservants serve out of a voluntary love, and therefore can be trusted, as Paul was entrusted with the gospel to the Gentile Nations.

This is just a simple concept, I know, but again, one that we lack the societal context for. There is nothing beautiful about our modern concept of slavery, and as with so many other pictures of relationships within the scriptures, we must turn back the clock and enter into God's culture.

And now I want to tell you a story about Peter, one that is going to rock your world and teach you something about how our Heavenly Father feels about you. Actually, I'm going to tell you three stories about Peter because his impact on the world was greater than Paul's – we just don't see it until it is pointed out.

## Unclean or Common:  Peter's Revelation

A humbling thought -- the truth remains, even if we are ignorant of it. Sight exists, though the blind cannot perceive it. Sound exists, though the deaf cannot hear it. Evil exists, though we deny it. Good exists, apart from our attempts to define it. At the core of everything is absolute truth.

We try to come up with absolutes about people and groups, and we create labels because they give us the illusion of refuge. The defensive and the callous are apt to live within those absolutes they create about people. The defensive do it to protect themselves, and the callous do it to give themselves license to treat people according to their prejudices. How firmly rooted we are in absolutes tells us much about our character. But there is a balance that is needed to see each person as an entirely distinct individual -- totally unique and not easily definable. No one is easily defined, not really, and when we define them externally we deny them their very humanity.  We were taught that at the base of Mt Sinai when God refused to hold different people to different standards. At Sinai we saw that all men have the same rights to justice and to a Covenantal relationship with God, with certain rights and obligations.

We need balance.  We must see trends and yet ignore them, notice similarities yet disregard them. We cannot treat people like categories.

There are things that are true. God is true, absolutely true. God is the bedrock of truth, the source and definition of all that is true. But people are more complicated than that -- we are true and false. Seeing people as they are requires stepping out of our comfort zone and not pre-judging or pre-defining. All that presumption ever amounts to is our trying to get a handle on how we think we should feel about them and how we think we should treat them (or as I describe it, getting our excuses lined up like little ducks in a row).

The most notable scriptural example is Peter's vision in Acts 10. All his life he had been trained to categorize all Gentiles as common if they were living according to the commandments (as opposed to holy, or set apart), and unclean if they were not living according to the commandments. This doctrine was so deeply ingrained that no one was preaching the gospel to the world (as commanded by Jesus[83]) because they didn't want to have anything to do with anything or anyone considered unclean for fear of becoming defiled. The LORD had to get Peter's attention, because the situation was unacceptable.

And so Peter was given a vision about a similar oral tradition, one that operated by the exact same halachic principle. In his vision a sheet was lowered containing "all manner of four-footed beasts" or in other words, both clean and unclean animals according to Lev 11. Sheep, cows, goats, deer, pigs, camels, horses, etc. A voice told Peter to "rise and eat." So why didn't he simply rise and eat the sheep, cow, goat or deer? They were clean, after all, and there was no reason not to. Why did Peter reply, "**Not so, Lord; for I have never eaten anything that is** *common or unclean.*"

Halachic laws said that when a clean animal, like a sheep, is touched by an unclean animal, like a pig – that the sheep is now "common" and therefore inedible! Nowhere in God's laws does it say this – what was made to be received with thanksgiving as food, is clean regardless of whatever other living animal touches it! So when God told Peter, "Rise and Eat," He wasn't changing the law, nor was he telling Peter to sin. He was telling him that the halachic law was ***wrong.*** He wasn't saying "eat the pig," He was saying something like, "Oh for Pete's sake, eat the sheep that was touched by the pig and stop being such a big baby about it!" And He told him three times. This wasn't just one, but two repetitions, so we know that this was a big deal to God.

Well sadly, the same halachic law applied to any association between Gentiles and Jews. No matter how well a Gentile kept the law, he was considered contaminated – unless he officially became a Jew, subjecting himself to the authority of the teachings (laws) of the elders. But Peter was still puzzled (remember what I said about conditioning?) until God

---

[83] Matt 28:19-20

sent him to the house of a Law-abiding Gentile named Cornelius.[84] When the Holy Spirit fell on the household of Gentiles, Peter finally made the connection.

*Acts 10:34-35 Then Peter opened his mouth, and said, Of a truth I perceive that God is no respecter of persons: But **in every nation he that feareth him, and worketh righteousness, is accepted with him**.*

Do you see how big this was? Peter felt comfortable with those unbiblical standards, so much so that the gospel was going no further than to the Jews, even after at least a decade. What Jesus showed him, through the vision, was that there are no clear-cut categories of people as he had been taught, and that each man must be seen with respect to his relationship with God. Peter had been willing to deny a relationship with God through Jesus to the Gentiles, because of doctrinal traditions unsupported by scripture. And it wasn't because he was heartless, or being purposefully racist – he just wasn't questioning what he had always accepted as truth.

Acts 10 boils down to one thing, and it isn't food. Acts 10 is a divine rebuke against *anyone* making personal judgments about who can and cannot have a relationship with God as a full citizen of the nation of Israel. We don't get to make that call, praise God, nor should we.

I had a dream many years ago, a rebuke. I and a bunch of other fairly normal-seeming people were living in a hospital. As I was wandering around visiting people in their rooms, I passed a nurse's station, where the medical staff had barricaded themselves. I saw a nurse, totally disgusted, saying, "Well, I think a person should get to choose who their brothers and sisters are!"

I looked at her and said, "Well, I am an adoptive mother and I assure you that if my husband and I adopt again, our sons will not be consulted! It is the job of the parents to build a family, whether the children approve or not!"

---

[84] Acts 10:2

I woke up and groaned, because I was guilty. I wanted to control the constituency of the Body of Christ just as bad as everyone else does, but as a child I lack the wisdom and compassion to make the right choices. I would much rather barricade myself away from the sick people. But Jesus said that it is the sick, and not the healthy, that need a physician. I need a physician, and I would rather mingle with my fellow patients who know they belong in a hospital than with the people who believe they are perfect. Jesus came to heal people like me and knit us together as a family of equals. Only Messiah has that kind of authority, to reach to the four corners of the Earth, and bring the Word of God and righteousness to the Gentiles. It is a testimony of the love of God that He has waited for the prophesied fullness of the Gentiles to come in to the family before returning. It is the act of a Father putting His family together.

## Working Righteousness

For all my Christian life, I was taught that I had "the righteousness of Christ." Imagine my shock in seeing that the phrase "righteousness of Christ" isn't even in the Bible anywhere. I was utterly floored.

What I found instead is that we have a righteousness *of* God, *through faith* in Christ.

*Ro 3:22 Even the **righteousness of God** which is by faith of Jesus Christ unto all and upon all them that believe: for there is no difference:*

*2 Cor 5:21 For he hath made him to be sin for us, who knew no sin; that we might be made the **righteousness of God** in him.*

*Phil 3:9 And be found in him, not having mine own righteousness, which is of the law, but that which is through the faith of Christ, the **righteousness which is of God** by faith*

The righteousness that is of God comes through faith in Christ, not giving us His perfection, but placing us in right standing with respect to having placed our faith in Jesus as the Son of God, the promised Messiah – placing us into Covenant through His shed blood. That faith, according to James 2:20, without works to prove it, is a dead faith. As we saw in the last chapter, Peter made a proclamation concerning those who would be accepted by God.

*Acts 10:34-35 Then Peter opened his mouth, and said, Of a truth I perceive that God is no respecter of persons: But **in every nation he that feareth him, and worketh righteousness, is accepted with him**.*

It is not by genetics, but through faith in Jesus (who had just been preached to Cornelius' household), and the *working* of righteousness.

In other words, righteousness is not just some ethereal concept, but something that is done.  So how does the Word define righteousness?

Tzedakah, from the root Tzadak, is the Hebrew word translated righteousness.  Everywhere it is used in the Word it designates the integration of belief and action, faith and works.

Genesis 15:6 – God told Abraham to look to the stars and made him a promise.  Abraham obeyed and believed and it was counted as a righteous act.

Gen 30:33 – Jacob told Laban to test his righteousness in action, according to what kinds of goats he was keeping for himself from the flock, according to their agreement.

Lev 19:15 – the Israelites were commanded to judge righteously in action.

Deut 9:5-6 – the Israelites were told that they were not being given the Land because of their righteous actions, but because of the unrighteous actions of the Canaanites.

Deut 33:19 – the sacrifices were called righteous actions.

Over and over again, throughout the Torah and the Prophets and the New Testament, righteousness is equated with doing something concrete in obedience.  The righteousness that we have of God by faith in Christ would therefore obligate us to  honor the teachings of Christ (after all, how can we say we have faith in Him if we do not do what He says?).  Christ taught that love towards God is evidenced by obedience to the commandments.  We prove that our faith is not dead through obedience, through works -- not works *for* salvation but as a natural outpouring of love and belief and acceptance of our position in the family of God.  Through doing His works of righteousness, performing acts of justice and charity, we honor Him in the eyes of the world as being King above all kings and Lord above all lords.

I want to wrap this up by quoting one of my favorite passages of scripture.

Deut 6:20-25 *And when thy son asketh thee in time to come, saying, What mean the testimonies, and the statutes, and the judgments, which the LORD our God hath commanded you?*

*Then thou shalt say unto thy son, We were Pharaoh's bondmen in Egypt; and the LORD brought us out of Egypt with a mighty hand:*

*And the LORD shewed signs and wonders, great and sore, upon Egypt, upon Pharaoh, and upon all his household, before our eyes:*

*And he brought us out from thence, that he might bring us in, to give us the land which he sware unto our fathers.*

**And the LORD commanded us to do all these statutes, to fear the LORD our God, for our good always,** *that he might preserve us alive, as it is at this day.*

**And it shall be our righteousness, if we observe to do all these commandments before the LORD our God, as he hath commanded us.**

Faith always has been and always will be evidenced by works of obedience, as our Master and His disciples taught.[85]

---

[85] John 14:15-24; I John 5:2-3

## How Peter's Vision Changed the World

As I already pointed out, at the time that Peter had his Acts 10 vision, God-fearing Jews were not permitted to enter the homes of Gentiles, even Gentiles who kept the commandments and worshiped the LORD. No eating with them, no drinking with them -- not until they underwent formal conversion to Judaism through circumcision -- which, for a Gentile in Roman times, was an act of treason against the Caesars, the choosing of another King, and another God (the Imperial Cult of Rome worshiped the Caesars as gods). The Jews were excluded because they chose to pay extra taxes, but no one else was getting away with it. Hence, we see Cornelius and his entire household keeping the commandments but uncircumcised. He was well spoken of by the Jews, but still an outsider. Peter's vision changed that, taking the faith of the followers of Jesus back to Sinai, so to speak, where there was no dividing line between natural born Israelite and those of the Nations who chose to live by the Covenant. People were to be judged not by the dictates of rabbinical halakah, but according to their faith as evidenced by their obedience to what is written.  Especially not, in this case, by halakah which were entirely unsupported by scripture and even broke scripture.

And so the decision of the Acts 15 council represents a colossal change of heart, I mean, truly breathtaking. Their decision comes down to a simple revelation -- people entering into the Covenant must have an opportunity to learn to live it.  And without the synagogues of the day, it was not going to happen. These people had no scriptures on their shelves at home, and even a wealthy man would not have an entire library of the Torah and the Prophets. For those of the Nations entering into the assembly of Israel, they had to learn from the Jews -- or they couldn't learn anything at all.

These learned men, filled with genuine love and compassion for the converting Gentiles, simply said, "You have to learn somewhere, come and join us, but you have to give up your idol worship completely. No drinking the blood of the sacrifice, no strangling animals at a pagan altar, no sex with cult prostitutes, and no worship of anything except the God of Israel.[86] We will teach you everything else. Join us on the Sabbath; you are welcome; you don't have to have it all figured out right now. It's okay, we will teach you."

I mean, this was HUGE. This changed the world. This was an act of true love, mercy and compassion. This was the epitome of grace in action. Interestingly enough, the sins they absolutely forbade were the same ones that, in the Torah, provoked the wrath of God upon the entire Nation of Israel. Those were the sins responsible for plagues breaking out and people being destroyed. By focusing on these, they were setting a baseline requirement -- "Cross over and never cross back."

Those coming in from the Nations were going to learn not to lie, steal, covet, or seek out diviners and magicians.  They would be instructed to keep the Sabbaths and the other Feasts as they sat through the Torah cycles year after year, something that just takes time and repetition -- for all of us.

In some ways, what the Acts 15 council said was just reiterating what Joshua said

*Joshua 24*

*14 Now therefore fear the Lord, and serve him in sincerity and in truth: and put away the gods which your fathers served on the other side of the flood, and in Egypt; and serve ye the Lord.*

*15 And if it seem evil unto you to serve the Lord, choose you this day whom ye will serve; whether the gods which your fathers served that were on the other side of the flood, or the gods of the Amorites, in whose land ye dwell: but as for me and my house, we will serve the Lord.*

*16 And the people answered and said, God forbid that we should forsake the Lord, to serve other gods;*

---

[86] Acts 15:20-21

There is nothing new under the sun, nothing ever really changes. The character of God is eternal and uncompromising. He is just. He is loving. He is truly the perfect Father.

## Intermission: Salvation is Your Name

Every night I go to bed and spend a few hours praying, and in the morning I know what to write. This morning I did my writing and then got the kids up for school. I had the next chapter heading all ready to go – but all day as I went about homeschooling and cleaning and cooking a very nice chicken pot pie, I had a song of Joshua Aaron's running through my mind. Five hours later, I started wondering about it and after prayer, I decided to take the hint and write this chapter.

You know what is so truly wonderful about Hebrew names? Their meanings! Hebrew children were not named lightly, their names were chosen carefully by their parents so as to define the parameters and character of their lives. As Joshua Aaron so beautifully sings, the Name of our Lord and Master defined His mission.

*There is a Name I call upon*
*There is a Name by which I'm saved*
*Salvation is Your Name, Salvation is Your Name*

*There is a Lamb who bore our sins*
*He bled and died, so we could live!*
*Salvation is Your Name, Salvation is Your Name*

Take John the Baptist – his real name was Yohannan ben Zacharyah, and it meant "God is gracious." What a beautiful name for the man who was born to elderly parents and who was heralding the coming Messiah, the living proof of God's eternal grace. His name was given to his father as he served in the Temple on the day of Shavuot (aka Pentecost), the yearly feast celebrating the giving of the commandments on Mt Sinai, by the Angel of the LORD.

Take Jesus – whose real Name was Yeshua ben Yosef, also a Name given to His parents by an Angel. The short form of Yehoshua (Joshua), it means "YHVH is salvation" – but not only that, it sounds very similar to the word for salvation, yoshia. When the angel spoke to Mary, he basically said, "You shall name Him Yeshua, for He shall yoshia His people." Hebrew puns, gotta love them!

So that song, "Salvation is His Name," is exactly on point. When we say Yeshua, it is a statement of faith that the LORD is our salvation. I will never hate the name of Jesus, it is the name I called on and I was saved; however, what I was really calling upon was the authority of the only begotten Son of the living God, the Messiah of Israel who died to pay the penalty for my sins, was buried and rose three days and nights later – just as He said He would. When I called out to Jesus, I was pledging my faith that it was all true and that I was surrendering my life to His Lordship. As much as I cherish the name Jesus, it has no meaning apart from the authority we call on, and so now that I know the truth, I call Him by the Name given by the Angel of the LORD.

*At the Name of Yeshua (Jesus) every knee shall bow*
*And every tongue will confess that He is Lord!*

*Salvation is Your Name, Salvation is Your Name*
*Yeshua is Your Name, Yeshua is Your Name*

*Yeshua, Yeshua*[87]

I call upon Yeshua knowing that every time I speak that Name, it is a bold proclamation that YHVH is indeed my salvation. I consider it a privilege to call Him what His Heavenly Father, earthly parents, disciples, followers, and the angels called Him.

So if you don't mind, it has been really hard to remember to type out Jesus, and I am going to give my brains a break and use Yeshua from now on.

---

[87] *My heartfelt thanks to Joshua Aaron Manarchuck, who gave his permission for the song lyrics to be used here. Copyright: © 2006 WorshipinIsrael.com songs.*
*https://www.youtube.com/user/worshipinisrael*

I am also going to replace the word LORD, with YHVH, the Tetragrammaton that is written in the Hebrew Bible 6,828 times but was replaced by The LORD in our English Bibles. It is how He chose to reveal Himself, and so I love to use it. What I won't do is tell you how I pronounce it, because that is a whole other story and subject to so many debates that I will leave it to your own studies.

Thanks for bearing with my little interlude! How funny, the song stopped playing in my mind so I can sleep tonight! Praise YHVH!

Now back to our beloved brother Peter, who changed our lives.

## So If Peter Was So Great Then Why Did Paul Rebuke Him?

Well, Peter had earned it. We all earn a good old rebuke now and then and this one was a doozy.

Remember Peter's vision? Remember that before Peter's vision no observant Jew would be caught dead in the house of a commandment keeping Gentile, much less eat with them? Well, what Peter did in Galatia is something that we have all done in our lifetimes; he betrayed the truth in favor of keeping difficult people happy.

*Galatians 2:11-14 But when Peter was come to Antioch, I withstood him to the face, because he was to be blamed.* **For before that certain came from James, he did eat with the Gentiles: but when they were come, he withdrew and separated himself, fearing them which were of the circumcision.** *And the other Jews dissembled likewise with him; insomuch that Barnabas also was carried away with their dissimulation. But when I saw that they walked not uprightly according to the truth of the gospel, I said unto Peter before them all,* **If thou, being a Jew, livest after the manner of Gentiles, and not as do the Jews, why compellest thou the Gentiles to live as do the Jews?**

So first of all, what was the circumcision group? In context, they were those believing Jews who wrongly held to the rabbinic ruling that it was not enough for former Gentiles (yes former, and I will use Paul to prove it later) to become grafted into the Olive Tree of Israel through Messiah, and keep the Torah commandments. They also insisted that the former Gentiles must convert formally to Judaism and keep all of their rabbinical commandments too. In other words, it was not enough for them to live according to the Covenant, but they also had to join an exclusive club.

In the eyes of the circumcision group (who we run into in Acts 15, Romans and Galatians), the newcomers must become proselytes – which meant that they had to do things in the reverse order of the written word, the gospel. First circumcision, then baptism and then learn the commandments – just the opposite of Abraham, who learned to live the commandments for 24 years and only then was circumcised. This is also the opposite order of those who were born in the wilderness to the children of Israel. Moses never once circumcised anyone! Joshua 5:5 makes that clear – this was a generation of 40 years who learned to live the commandments first, and then passed through the Jordan River, and then were circumcised. Learning the walk always came before circumcision, unless you were born into the Covenant and, like Yeshua, circumcised on the 8th day.

You see, when one is born into the Covenant, they learn it by living it – which is relatively easy. This is why Paul said there was "every advantage" to having been born a Jew. But having lived all one's life apart from the Covenant and then having to learn it as an adult is quite the challenge. The Jerusalem council righteously and compassionately pointed out that it was best to allow the incoming Gentiles to learn to live the commandments in the synagogues each Sabbath, and then allow them to decide when they wanted to submit to the final step of circumcision. After all, even their own forefathers had never had to bear the kind of burden that the "circumcision group" was trying to place on the incoming Gentile believers.

Now, before the vision from Heaven, Peter was not yet willing to die to his doctrinal prejudices and go preach to the Gentiles. And before his encounter with Paul in Galatia, he was not willing to die at the hands of the few religious bullies who came from James – not socially or otherwise. He didn't want to rock the boat, even though he was the one who knew better than anyone how YHVH felt about the former Gentiles!

Peter's entire ministry was preparing him to die. Peter had once boldly proclaimed he would gladly die for Yeshua, even if everyone else left Him. And I bet he believed it, I don't think he was lying. I mean, we all believe we can do it, until it is revealed otherwise. But Peter wasn't really willing to die yet, and that had to change because Peter was going to end up crucified for Messiah.

Gal 2:11-14 didn't happen in a cafeteria, with a popular kids table and a nerd table. It happened with the Jews keeping to Jewish homes and the Gentiles now eating in Gentile homes, and of all people on earth, Peter knew better (Acts 10). Peter was observing rabbinical halakah, which ordained that no Jew could eat with a Gentile, or in their home, period, or their food would be defiled. This means that he was no longer breaking bread with the former Gentile believers because they had not formally submitted to rabbinic authority. This was a grievous error.

Why? Because Peter was not willing, in this matter, to take up the cross of Yeshua and die to self for the former Gentiles, nor was he willing to die to self for the handful of Jewish believers who came from James. They were sinning and getting away with it! In allowing this, he risked killing both groups in order to please men, but not all men, just the men who were in the wrong. He was undoing the work of Messiah by not teaching it with his actions, and was therefore living like an uncovenanted Gentile, in sin, even as he was telling the former Gentiles to live like Jews, according to Torah. In other words, he was telling the former Gentiles to live righteously while he was not because of fear, just like the night of Yeshua's arrest.

Many of us, like Peter, have shown preferential love to the wrong people. Preferential love directed at the wrong is detestable. We are not to love them more by showing favoritism -- that is abuse mentality. That is the state of mind that says, "Everyone has to walk on eggshells around the abuser so maybe he will be nice to us." Who in their right mind wants to be the "nice kid" who the bully tolerates while he is busy beating up all the other kids? That nice kid is only friends with himself, in the end -- not willing to suffer or die for anyone or anything. And he probably tells himself he is a light in the life of that bully, but he isn't. At most he's just a slightly lighter shade of darkness.

Peter didn't have to go looking for a fight, he didn't have to go looking for a way to be offensive, and he didn't have to go get into anyone's business. He was already neck deep in a silent fight, and it was already offensive, and the very people he was trying to please had already made it his business. He didn't have to be hateful -- he just had to be willing to die to self in order to fight the hatred that was already there.

In the end, Peter did die to himself and repent, which is why I love him so dearly.

## On the Subject of Gentiles and Former Gentiles

This one came as quite the shock to me! I read it so many times, but I never saw it – perhaps because I had been told I was a Gentile so many times that I ignored all scriptural evidence to the contrary!

*Ephesians 2:11-19 Wherefore remember, that **ye being in time past Gentiles** in the flesh, who are called Uncircumcision by that which is called the Circumcision in the flesh made by hands; that at that time ye were without Christ, **being aliens from the commonwealth of Israel**, and **strangers from the covenants** of promise, having no hope, and **without God** in the world: But now in Christ Jesus ye who sometimes were far off are made nigh by the blood of Christ. For he is our peace, **who hath made both one, and hath broken down the middle wall of partition** between us; having **abolished** in his flesh the enmity, even **the law of commandments contained in ordinances**; for to make in himself of twain one new man, so making peace; and that he might reconcile both unto God in one body by the cross, having slain the enmity thereby: And came and preached peace to you which were afar off, and to them that were nigh. For through him we both have access by one Spirit unto the Father. Now therefore **ye are no more strangers and foreigners, but fellow citizens with the saints, and of the household of God;***

So according to Paul, we are no longer to call ourselves Gentiles but instead fellow citizens with the saints, the household of YHVH, the commonwealth of Israel! If we do a reverse on what this says, we can get a biblical definition of the word Gentile.

Gentile – without Messiah, aliens from the commonwealth of Israel, stranger to the covenants (plural), without hope, without God, not saints, not members of the household of God.

Good grief, who would want to be identified as a Gentile after seeing that! That's just wretched!

What we are called to become is not a bunch of Gentile believers, because according to Paul, there is no such thing. We instead become Israelites, just like the Jews, grafted into that same Olive Tree of Romans 11, spoken of by the prophet Jeremiah, whose branches were broken because the people broke the Covenant.[88]

Interesting side note here – we have been talking about Peter's vision and the rabbinical halakah that separated Jew from Gentile and you can see it all over this passage. Look at that "middle wall of partition" – that isn't Biblical; that's rabbinical halakah, the exact same ones I have been writing about. And what did Yeshua do? He abolished the *law of commandments contained in ordinances*, referring directly back to what? That wall of separation between Jew and former Gentile that is found nowhere in the law as given to Moses and therefore cannot be referring to the Torah, which always treated Israelites and foreigners with equality. In the Torah, there was no enmity when a foreigner would come and sojourn with Israel to worship YHVH; that never existed until after the Babylonian exile and the rise of the Oral Law, as Jews were desperately trying to retain their national identity by repelling the influence of Greek and then Roman culture (and I can honestly see why it happened – they did not want to make the same mistake twice and fall into paganism and exile). But in so doing, they were completely denying their own culture – based on the Word of YHVH. Without the tearing down of that middle wall of separation, Yeshua could not fulfill the Messianic expectation that Messiah would bring the Torah to the Nations, as prophesied by Isaiah

*2:2 And it shall come to pass **in the last days**, that the mountain of the LORD'S house shall be established in the top of the mountains, and shall be exalted above the hills; and **all nations shall flow unto it**.*

---

[88] Jer 11:16-17

*3 And many people shall go and say, Come ye, and let us go up to the mountain of the LORD, to the house of the God of Jacob; and **he will teach us of his ways**, and we will walk in his paths: **for out of Zion shall go forth the law**, and the word of the LORD from Jerusalem.*

## The Parable of the Rebellious Houseguest

A lot of times we make the mistake of thinking that a rebellious person is mean or spiteful or purposefully being destructive. But the truth of the matter is that your garden variety rebel is no different than we are, as seen through the eyes of God. I'm going to teach you about all of us by telling you a parable.

One of the ways that Messiah was to be identified was through the teaching of parables. Many think that Yeshua was unique in teaching with parables, but in fact many in the Bible used them, from the false prophet Balaam to Job and the prophets. Parables were a recognized Hebrew teaching method, using stories to relate a larger truth. In a way, I see it as another reflection of God as our Father. After all, how many of us have told the parable of the boy who cried wolf to teach our children not to lie in order to get attention? It is easier for children to learn when they have a concrete story. That being said, the parables of the Bible are not always easy to understand – even Yeshua's own disciples had to ask Him for interpretations! Mine are not as deep as His, and so you won't struggle, unless I do a bad job of telling it!

Once upon a time there was a woman who asked to come live with a family. She had been having hard times and the family took her in with the plans that she would get healthy, get a steady job, become whole emotionally and spiritually, and learn to live in such a way that would be beneficial to herself and everyone in her life.

The couple really liked her. She was an outgoing, nice person with a great sense of humor but there were also some problems when she got to their home. She had a problem with her foot which made it difficult for her to walk at times, but that was okay. The wife of the house rubbed essential oils on her foot and prayed over her and after about two weeks it was healed up.

When it came to doing things for herself, she did great. She started on the treadmill and got healthier. She spent a lot of time reading the scriptures and listening to teachings. But when it came to living according to the rules everyone else lived by, the problems started to surface. She would eat what was for dinner, unless she didn't like it and then she made something for herself with whatever she wanted to use, really blowing the food budget. She refused to follow the rules about not having coffee in carpeted areas, which resulted in a stain on the carpet. After being confronted, she told the hosts that she thought the rules were only for the kids, even though they had been spoken directly to her. Instead of obeying the rules, she found a travel mug and went where she pleased with it. And there were many little ways that she refused to live like a member of the household, causing problems with keeping the children of the house in line. The kids wanted to know why she lived like she wanted in their home when they couldn't. It was also difficult on the couple. Discipline really broke down, and life became more and more difficult day by day. She was resentful, and they became resentful as well.

They worked with her to get her a job for weeks, driving her around for applications and interviews. When she got a job they drove her to and from work, but she quit after a short time and announced her desire to go somewhere else. They bought her a plane ticket and sent her on her way.

Now how does this apply to us? Well, when we say yes to adoption, we are joining a family. We are not guests and we have no right to act like we are living in a hotel where we make up our own rules. Our Father made up the rules, and they are the same for everyone. Can you imagine living in a house where different people are held to different standards based on what they think they should do, based on their definition of right and wrong? It sounds like living in a house with a bunch of teenagers! Forever!

130

The truth is that rebellion doesn't require ill intentions; rebellion just means that we don't accept any rulership over us. It means that we don't respect the authority of the head of the house to make rules for us to live by. You can be happy-go-lucky and be completely rebellious; you don't have to have a mean bone in your body.

There is an attitude that we grew up with in church that Is very rebellious indeed. We were taught that we are entitled to all the blessings of God without the curses (discipline) that come as a natural consequence of our actions. In other words, we were taught that we had the right to be spoiled brats, to be given everything we wanted and held to no standards except those that we or our denominations approved of. We developed the attitude that we deserved the perks that came with good works, without having to do any of the good works. Honestly, that pretty much sounds like the average child these days.

The truth is that we never had the right to expect any goodies from our Heavenly Father without obedience. What kind of Father would hand out incentives to disobey?

Through comparing the Body of Messiah to a family, He is showing us a larger picture of how he sees things. I once heard a teacher say, "God is preparing us to be the kind of people He wants to spend eternity with." Wow. Yes, it is true and scriptures tell us about the preparation of the Bride – but each Bride must start out as a child. Our lives on this planet are spent as the children of God preparing to be the pure and spotless Bride of Messiah.

So how does this situation relate to how a child ought to conduct themselves if they wants to become the kind of person whom God wants to spend eternity with? After all, like the houseguest, we all come into this with problems with our "walk," with how we do things in order to live a life that is both pleasing to God and respectful towards others.  He expects us to come into all this woefully disabled, but He also expects our cooperation so that we won't stay that way.  He works diligently with us to heal us so that we can walk in more and more harmony with Him and He expects us to be grateful and respond with obedience and trust so that He can continue to bless us.

When we become part of the household of God, there are rules and regulations that apply to everyone. No different from our own houses, so again God uses the familiar to teach us about the spiritual.  We have a choice as to how to respond to the rules of any house.  We can obey them and recognize the authority of the Master of the house, we can assume they are only meant for others, or we can resent the rules and disobey them or find ways around them.  When everyone in the house obeys the rules, life is good and there is peace and a feeling of comfortableness and love thrives.  When some decide the rules don't apply to them, resentment brews between the people who obey and those who disobey.  In this situation, there is neither peace nor comfortableness and love is choked off.  When someone decides to resent and break and circumvent the rules, life is awful for everyone and detrimental to the stability of the family.  The home ceases to be a home.  No one wants to live with a rebellious and resentful person.  When it is our child, we do our duty and continue to try, but when the person is an adult, there is no use living with them at all – knowing that their presence serves no purpose but to destroy the home for everyone else.

But there are people, who although they resent and disobey the rules, want and feel entitled to the blessings that come to those living in the home who are obedient.  Now, as parents, we know that it is a delight to reward obedient children, but that rewarding disobedience just creates more of a rebel.  Rewarding disobedience is not love, but instead hatred – setting the child up for a lifetime of thinking they should be rewarded for doing the wrong thing.  In the same way, our

Heavenly Father is both loving and compassionate, and by His very nature He cannot reward resentment and disobedience.

As Christians, we have been taught that we are deserving of the blessings of Deuteronomy 28 that were tied to obedience, without having to be obedient. We were also taught that we are free from all the curses of disobedience found in that same chapter – even though we see them increasingly happening all around us and to us.

I ask you, as a parent, what do you do to get your child's attention when they are going astray if you cannot discipline (curse) them? How do you get their attention to come back and do what is right? Well really, if your child is rebellious enough not to care about what you say, there is absolutely nothing you can do except to lift your hand and stop protecting them, just like YHVH did with the Northern Kingdom of Israel, and later the Southern Kingdom of Judah. He lifted His hand and allowed them to see what happens when they refuse to walk in obedience and blessings, and showed them everything He had protected them from, by allowing it to happen. He allowed them to experience what the pagan nations had to deal with on a regular basis. Now, isn't that what a good parent does to get their child's attention? Let them go to jail for their crimes, let them go bankrupt, let them reap what they have sown? Why do we so easily identify what makes people good parents and then say that God does not operate by the same principles, when in His word it clearly says that this is exactly how He operates.

And so, let us go back to the parable. The houseguest made her intentions clear through her actions that she did not want to live under the house rules and she was sent packing, even though she had asked to come and live there. I can't help think but this –

*Matthew 7*

*²¹ Not every one that saith unto me, Lord, Lord, shall enter into the kingdom of heaven; **but he that doeth the will of my Father** which is in heaven.*

*²² Many will say to me in that day, Lord, Lord, have we not prophesied in thy name? and in thy name have cast out devils? and in thy name done many wonderful works?*

*²³ And then will I profess unto them, **I never knew you: depart from me, ye that work iniquity.***

*²⁴ Therefore whosoever heareth these sayings of mine, and **doeth them**, I will liken him unto a wise man, which built his house upon a rock:*

What is the will of the Father? It has been stated in scripture over and over again – do His commandments, walk in all His ways. What does YHVH require of us? When we accept the blood of Yeshua, we are saying, "I want to live with You, please help me." When we refuse to abide by His commandments, we are telling Him that we want His help but that we don't want anything else. We want an anonymous benefactor; we don't really want to know Him.

*Micah 6:8 He hath shewed thee, O man, what is good; and what doth the LORD require of thee, but to do justly, and to love mercy, and to walk humbly with thy God?*

How can we do justly without following His system of justice as outlined in His laws? How can we do mercy if we do not allow Him to define it for us? How can we walk humbly with our God if we do not submit to His authority and call His laws good and agree to walk in them as He does? He does not break His own laws – how can we?

In Matt 7:22 we see one of the most well-known verses in the Bible. People who have been doing wonderful things in the Name of Messiah – these aren't unbelievers, but those who have been serving Him and fully expected to be told, "Well done good and faithful servant." They are even justifying themselves before God, much as Job did. But His response is that He never knew them, He calls them workers of iniquity.

Looks to me like we need to find out what iniquity is, so we don't end up trying to justify ourselves to YHVH after a lifetime of what we considered to be good works, only to be booted out for iniquity.

## What is Iniquity?

In light of the passage in Matthew, it behooves us to find out what iniquity is. In the Greek, the word translated iniquity is anomia, and according to Thayer's Greek Lexicon,[89] it means

1. The condition of one without law, either because ignorant of it, or because violating it
2. Contempt and violation of law, iniquity, wickedness

Other translations use the word "lawlessness" in place of anomia. I ask very genuinely, because I once had to ask myself this question – how can we be lawless when there is no more law?

I have already argued that the law was not whittled down to one or two commandments, but instead summarized. In addition, I have pointed out that if Messiah struck down the law He would not be Messiah, but instead a transgressor. I have also proven that Yeshua and the Father are One and in agreement about everything, and therefore the law must be forever, eternal and everlasting as declared by Moses, whose credentials Yeshua validated.

Iniquity then is lawlessness, and Yeshua clearly stated in Matthew 7:23 that those who have contempt for the law, who are without the law, are at risk of being told to depart, no matter how many miracles they have performed in His Name!

Because this is so vitally important, I am going to go through some of the anomia verses in the NT, the quotes are from the KJV, but I kept the Greek word anomia where appropriate.

---

[89] Thayer's Greek Lexicon, Electronic Database.
Copyright © 2002, 2003, 2006, 2011 by Biblesoft, Inc.

*Matt 13:41 The Son of man shall send forth his angels, and they shall **gather out of his kingdom** all things that offend, and **them which do anomia***

This verse is referring to the last days. This is about what happens well after He supposedly nailed the law to the cross. He will send His angels to gather those who practice lawlessness out of His Kingdom – not from Satan's kingdom, but out of His Kingdom. The righteous will remain, but the lawless will be gathered up.

*Matt 23:28 Even so ye also outwardly appear righteous unto men, but within ye are full of hypocrisy and **anomia.***

This was about some of the Pharisees, who found ways to circumnavigate the laws they didn't like. Even today, modern day Pharisees (Orthodox Jews) will often break the Passover commandment to rid our homes of leaven, to have none of it within our borders, by ceremonially renting out their leaven to Gentiles for a small fee for the duration of the week of Unleavened Bread.

*Matt 24:12 And because **anomia** shall abound, the love of many shall wax cold.*

Again, speaking of the last days, and the fact that lawlessness causes love to grow cold. What did John say?

*I John 2:3-4 And hereby we do know that we know him, if we keep his commandments. **He that saith, I know him, and keepeth not his commandments, is a liar,** and the truth is not in him.*

What did Yeshua say?

*John 14:15 and 21 **If ye love me, keep my commandments**. He that hath my commandments, and keepeth them, he it is that loveth me: and he* *that loveth me shall be loved of my Father, and I will love him, and will manifest myself to him.*

What did Moses say?

*Deut 11:1 Therefore thou shalt love the L*ORD *thy God, and **keep his charge, and his statutes, and his judgments, and his commandments, always.***

Love is proven by obedience, and through doing what is pleasing to the person we love, and when we do not obey, our hearts naturally stop loving. We become cold, for only coldness will keep us from serving those we love.

*Romans 6:19 I speak after the manner of men because of the infirmity of your flesh: for as ye have yielded your members servants to uncleanness and to **anomia unto anomia**; even so now yield your members servants to righteousness unto holiness.*

Paul says here that men who are ruled by the flesh, through lawlessness, give themselves over as servants to lawlessness. Paul, like Yeshua and Moses, commands us to give ourselves over to the opposite – righteousness unto set-apartness. We yield our members over not just to righteous thoughts or intentions, but righteous action unto holiness, set-apartness.

*I Cor 6:14-15 Be ye not unequally yoked together with unbelievers: **for what fellowship hath righteousness with anomia**? and what communion hath light with darkness? And what concord hath Christ with Belial? or what part hath he that believeth with an infidel?*

Again we see that righteousness is at odds with lawlessness. Lawlessness is equated with darkness and all things evil and corrupt and idolatrous in the verses that follow.

*2 Thess 2:7 For the mystery of anomia doth already work: only he who now letteth will let, until he be taken out of the way.*

As we can see, again, from Paul – lawlessness was already at work during his days, both in mainstream Judaism (especially among the Sadducees) as well as in the assembly of believers in Yeshua, as Paul's letters to the Corinthians tells us!

*I John 3:4* **Whoever commits sin commits anomia: for sin is anomia** (substitutions mine, based on the Greek)

Whoever sins is practicing lawlessness, because sin is lawlessness.

Lawlessness is serious business, but we have had it drilled into our heads all our lives that Yeshua did it all so we don't have to do anything. We were told that since we have the Holy Spirit, we are able to determine all things that are right and wrong and yet we see believers in the pew and pulpit committing monstrous acts of lawlessness, not only according to God's righteous standard, but even according to the standards of the world.

How did this happen?  The same exact way it happened in ancient Israel; people got prosperous they stopped obeying God, their love grew cold and they started doing terrible, idolatrous, lawless things.  Nothing ever changes – look around.  Are we reaping the promised blessings of Deuteronomy 28, or are we living with the curses?  Are we sick, barren, and lacking financially?  Are we exhausted?  Are we borrowers or lenders? Are we at war, or peace?  Are our religious leaders in the news for the good they do, or because of the crimes they commit (often the crimes their congregations excuse and turn a blind eye to)? Do we stand as a united front against the darkness, or are we simply a lighter shade of darkness? We can all see that we are living in the last days – the world needs us to be light and to be set apart.  We can all see that our way simply is not working.  As a result, we have reached an era where believers are not hated for the sake of His Name; instead He is hated for our sake.  Indeed, we have corporately broken the third commandment by bringing His Name to shame in the eyes of the world.  We have also corporately broken the fifth commandment by not honoring Him as a Father should be honored.

Are you practicing anomia in ignorance? I know I was. Are you tired of walking in the curses like the prodigal son? Are you ready to turn around, run home, and do things our Father's way?

Anomia is at the heart of a very important concept in Revelation – the Mark of the Beast, but first, let us look at the Mark of God.

## The Sign of God vs. the Mark of the Beast

Three times in the Torah, a sign is referenced as being on the back of the hand and between the eyes.

*Ex 13:9 And it shall be for **a sign unto thee upon thine hand, and for a memorial between thine eyes**, that the LORD's law may be in thy mouth: for with a strong hand hath the LORD brought thee out of Egypt.*

*Deut 6:8 And thou shalt bind them for a **sign upon thine hand, and they shall be as frontlets between thine eyes**.*

*Deut 11:18 Therefore shall ye lay up these my words in your heart and in your soul, and **bind them for a sign upon your hand, that they may be as frontlets between your eyes**.*

That should look very much like another three references from Revelation, because it is supposed to look like it. Nothing is haphazardly phrased in the prophetic writings.

*Rev 13:16 And he causeth all, both small and great, rich and poor, free and bond, to receive **a mark in their right hand, or in their foreheads**:*

*Rev 14:9-10 And the third angel followed them, saying with a loud voice, If any man worship the beast and his image, and **receive his mark in his forehead, or in his hand,** The same shall drink of the wine of the wrath of God, which is poured out without mixture into the cup of his indignation; and he shall be tormented with fire and brimstone in the presence of the holy angels, and in the presence of the Lamb:*

*Rev 20:4 And I saw thrones, and they sat upon them, and judgment was given unto them: and I saw the souls of them that were beheaded for the witness of Jesus, and for the word of God, and which had not worshipped the beast, neither his image, neither had **received his mark upon their foreheads, or in their hands**; and they lived and reigned with Christ a thousand years.*

If you look at the Sign of YHVH and the Mark of the Beast side by side, you will see a similar theme. The Sign of God is tied in to obedience – and so is the Mark of the Beast. The Sign of God is specifically tied to obedience to His laws, and the Mark of the Beast is tied to obedience to the Beast's laws. We must ask ourselves why this is included in scripture, the Sign of God, if not to protect us from the Mark of the Beast, as nothing is in scripture randomly or lightly.

I can only come up with one reason – and it is simply that without obedience to the laws of God, we may take the Mark of the Beast without even realizing it. Let's face it, even most unbelievers are adverse to 666 tattoos or RFID chips in general. People are expecting the Mark to look like that. But what if the Beast's laws simply outlaw those portions of the laws of God that Christians have already been told are done away with, and the Mark of the Beast isn't any more external than the Sign of God? That should be a terrifying thought.

If that is the case, since Revelation is a Book about a Bride, perhaps we should find out how being a bride ties in to the picture.

## Who is the Bride?

*Rev 19:7-9 Let us be glad and rejoice, and give honour to him: for the marriage of the Lamb is come, and **his wife hath made herself ready.***

*[8] And to her was granted that she should be arrayed in fine linen, clean and white: for the fine linen is the **righteousness of saints.***

*[9] And he saith unto me, Write, Blessed are they which are called unto the marriage supper of the Lamb. And he saith unto me, These are the true sayings of God.*

Contrary to popular doctrine, not everyone will be the Bride. In fact, those who believe that they need nothing more than a confessed faith in Messiah will be lucky to be wedding guests, according to Yeshua Himself.

In the parable of the wedding banquet of Matthew 22, Yeshua speaks of those who are invited to the wedding of the King's son (referring to Himself). There are three groups

1. The people who were invited but either would not come, or mocked the King, or killed his servants.
2. Those who were gathered, "both bad and good," who came
3. The man who was gathered but did not have the proper garment and was thrown out.

By definition, there are three others – the King, the Bridegroom and the Bride.

The first group were called, but refused to come. The second group were the good and bad who were gathered AND came dressed appropriately (to some extent, they had prepared, but were both "bad and good" – a combination that has been clearly spelled out as unacceptable since the Garden). The third group represented those who came to the party but had not done anything but show up "just as they are."

The King is God the Father, the Bridegroom is Yeshua, and the Bride is the woman who has made *herself* ready. The guests did and did not make themselves ready, to varying degrees.

But the Bride has labored to make herself completely ready. Her husband-to-be ransomed her, and it was her only purpose after that day, to get *herself* ready to be *His* bride.

But how is a woman supposed to know how to make her husband happy? How does she make herself ready?

That's where the Ketubah, the marriage covenant, comes in. The Ketubah is something that is still a beautiful part of Jewish culture, and a good thing too – because much of the Bible is written in Ketubah language. Just another way that the Jews have preserved the oracles of God in writing and in action!

## The Ketubah (or everything you ever wanted to know about making Him happy)

Much of the Bible is written from the point of view of the next relationship we are going to delve into – the marriage relationship. As we educate ourselves to the beauty of how weddings were organized and conducted, we begin to see how the Father meant to train us as children, for the sole purpose of being eternally wedded to His Son.

When a young man wanted to marry a woman, he would go, with his father, to the door of the young woman's house and knock. If she expressed her approval, her father would open the door and they would eat together. Perhaps now this missive to the Laodicean church is making more sense –

*Rev 3:20 Behold, I stand at the door, and knock: if any man hear my voice, and open the door, I will come in to him, and will sup with him, and he with me.*

The Laodiceans were so lukewarm, that they hadn't even opened the door yet! They were going through the motions, but were unwilling to allow either the Father or the Bridegroom in! Imagine being lukewarm about the opportunity to be wedded to the Son of the Living God! To be lukewarm is not the same as hatred, it is worse than hatred – to be lukewarm means that you just don't care at all.

To illustrate, there were three groups of believers living in the Nazi occupation during WWII. The first group was cold; they hated the Jews, and by extension hated God. Their hatred made them murderers, if only by consent. The second group was hot, and they risked their lives and families to protect Jewish families. Their love for God was proven by their righteous works of love towards their neighbors. The third group was the largest, the lukewarm. They simply did not care. People were rounded up into ghettos, and they did not care. People started disappearing from the ghettos and still they did not care. Caring results in action, otherwise it is nothing more than a vague sense of guilt. This is why YHVH hates the lukewarm and will spit them out of His mouth. He has no desire for a Bride who is indifferent. No man wants that kind of bride!

Now let us get back to the wedding arrangements. After they shared a meal with salt, they would get to the work of the Ketubah, the bridal Covenant. Once the Covenant was ratified by two witnesses, the couple was legally married, but the marriage would not be consummated until the bridegroom had gone back to his father's house to prepare a room for them to live in. He would literally build on to his father's house. Mary and Joseph were in this transitional phase when she was impregnated by the Holy Spirit. They were engaged and Joseph would have been in the process of providing a place for them to live together after the formal ceremony. That piece of information should make this verse make more sense.

*John 14:2-3 In my Father's house are many mansions: if it were not so, I would have told you. I go to prepare a place for you.*

*And if I go and prepare a place for you, I will come again, and receive you unto myself; that where I am, there ye may be also.*

Have you ever wondered why the 10 virgins were waiting for the bridegroom?[90] It's because the betrothal was done, and he had gone off to prepare a room in his father's house!

Five were wise and five were foolish, but they all fell asleep. Five prepared themselves and five did not. The ones who did not prepare were shut out of the wedding chamber – they would not be the bride – even though they were virgins! They all had a measure of hope, in that

---

[90] Matt 25

they waited, but five did not have the faith to get themselves ready, and by the time they realized they had to – it was too late.

The structure of the Ketubah is fascinating, and a prophetic picture of what we are to do to prepare ourselves in hopes of being the Bride. It was divided into five sections, just like the five books of the law as given to Moses. Within it is a detailed account of who the Bridegroom is, who the Bride is, the story of how they met, what the Bride's obligations are and what the Bridegroom's obligations are. The fifth section is signed off on by two witnesses – representing Moses and Elijah, the Torah and the Prophets. To this day, Jewish couples still covenant with each other in this beautiful, prophetic way.

The Bride had a certain amount of time, often a year, to learn her Covenant obligations – how to make her husband happy. But since she didn't know how long it would take, she had to work diligently to get ready as soon as possible! The Ketubah would teach her what he did and did not like, and what pleased and displeased him. His Covenant obligations were to protect and bless her and not forsake her unless she broke the covenant through adultery. Each one had very specific duties which they were to take very seriously. The Bride MUST learn to please her husband, and the Bridegroom MUST love, honor, protect and bless her. This was not a one-sided form of slavery, everyone had obligations. And might I add that these were not burdensome obligations – who wouldn't love to have a written record of exactly what their future spouse loves and hates?

It comes down to this – when we truly love someone, when we want to become one with them, we want to know what makes them happy and unhappy, we want to know what foods they love and hate, we want to know how to please them. Making them happy makes us happy, if we love them.

And we haven't been left as orphans, without instruction as to how to make our Bridegroom happy, we were given the Torah, which contains detailed instructions to help us become a suitable helpmeet for the eternal Bridegroom, a Bride He would delight in having because of the love and respect she shows for His Father.  Through it, we learn what He loves, and hates, what is clean and unclean, set apart, and detestable, food and not food, when to celebrate, when to rest, when to work, how to treat people and most importantly how to love Him by keeping all these instructions He provided, not because He wants us to fail, but because He wants us to succeed.  We learn how to be a holy Bride, because He is a holy Bridegroom.  We want to render Him honor by preparing ourselves, showing the world that He is worth our utmost.

And if people like Zechariah and Elizabeth succeeded without the Holy Spirit, just think of what we are capable of with the Holy Spirit.

There is no time to lose, the five wise virgins made preparations, even though they had fallen asleep for a time.  Never assume it is too late, even if you have fallen asleep and you are feeling a bit groggy.  Please don't give yourself cause to regret by not trying.

And please, please don't waste any time being angry.

## The Snare of Anger

When people learn the truth about the law still being in full effect, and about its purpose, they are often filled with joy and even relief and then anger when others don't understand. Joy is good; it propels us forward, while anger always has us looking back, turning disapproving eyes on those whose eyes have not yet been opened. Such anger is not in keeping with good fruit, and is generally counterproductive. We never know when our last day upon the earth is, so please do not waste a moment on the "what ifs" or the "why aren't they" thoughts but turn your heart to gratitude and joy that you know the truth while there is still time to prepare.

I guess what I am saying is, don't waste a moment recreating my mistakes when you can learn from them. I will share my testimony at the end of the book, but I want to give you the ugly story behind the testimony.

I learned the truth when God spoke to me about a certain behavior and challenged me to justify it scripturally and I couldn't. He called it an abomination in the Torah and in the Prophets, but I had made a bunch of New Testament verses mean what I wanted them to mean – or really, I just listened to what my pastors said. I repented with weeping, but then I had great joy as He started opening up the scriptures for me and I started seeing what was and was not good as He would personally challenge different areas in my life. I wasn't unhappy because I wasn't losing anything worth having. I shared with others what was happening, and the miracles I was experiencing, expecting them to have an "aha" moment, but they called me names, taking scripture out of context in order to do to me exactly what I used to do to others.

And I was angry at them and I judged them – for the crime of doing exactly what I had done a short time before! I was so arrogant, not to mention ungrateful. My excitement and gratitude were eaten away by my unrighteous anger. I mean really, how dare I judge people for merely being no different than I was? It wasn't like I figured it out for myself, with some sort of great intellectual prowess. No, YHVH showed me grace and mercy and opened my eyes, no differently than when He opened Paul's eyes on the road to Damascus. Should I yell at Paul for Yeshua not speaking to him earlier? Wouldn't I really just be judging Messiah for delaying the revelation of who He is? YHVH had His own reasons for delaying that revelation, and I do not judge Him. Nor do I judge Him for waiting in my case, or in yours or anyone's, but I waded through a lot of misplaced resentment first, resentment that led to some really bad fruit on my part and created unnecessary stumbling blocks for others. It's really quite embarrassing to think about the things I did.

I got involved with an online ministry where the preacher spent a lot of time yelling, and I got angrier (and more abusive to people who weren't "getting it") until one day I left (because he turned his disapproval on me) and found another teacher, one who was preparing people to be the Bride – with compassion, love, and firmness, and I began to undo the damage I had done to myself. I started to grow again, walking in the fullness that I was meant to walk in from the beginning. Since that day, I have grown more than I have grown my entire life, I am happy for the miracles, I am grateful to know what pleases my King, and I am relieved to know how to prepare myself in hope of being the Bride.

But in a way I am also grateful for my angry period – because I learned the difference between the letter and the Spirit of the law. The letter, as interpreted by that first teacher of mine, was killing me and others – one even denied Yeshua as Messiah a year ago. You can have Yeshua and you can have the law, but if you don't allow it to humble you and change you and transform you into a person who loves God and loves your neighbor, then the law does you no good at all. Don't waste time being set-apart only on the outside. Paul was set apart on the outside, and yet a murderer on the inside.

At the end of Exodus, we read about the building of the Tabernacle in the wilderness, where the true early church first gathered (Acts 7:38, yeah that shocked me too, I thought it began at Pentecost!). It is important to note, that the Tabernacle was set up from the inside out. The Tabernacle is a picture of the earthly dwelling of the Holy Spirit – us.

He builds us from the inside out in order to make a suitable habitation, according to the exact instructions of God. Just like the Tabernacle was built according to the exact instructions of God.

Don't waste time being angry at others. Don't waste time being angry at yourself. Be joyful and learn to be a lively stone in that living Tabernacle, be that purified Bride who has prepared herself. Come and prepare yourself to be a source of joy to the King! That is what I want for you – I want you to be the Bride, just like I want it for myself. There is no greater privilege than finding out that the entire Bible is your inheritance, and not divvied up among Jews and Gentiles, where we get this and they get that. So practice gratitude, practice joy, and fight that flesh!

## Learning How to Study the Scriptures

No amount of listening to teachings can ever replace actually sitting down and reading through the Bible over and over again. Unless we do, we will never know if the teachings are correct, and we will be at the mercy of men and whatever their blind spots and agendas are. We will be subject to the lies that they were taught by the men who lied to them because they were lied to by others who all genuinely thought that they were telling the truth. There is a verse about this –

*Jer 16:19 O LORD, my strength, and my fortress, and my refuge in the day of affliction, the Gentiles shall come unto thee from the ends of the earth, and shall say, **Surely our fathers have inherited lies, vanity, and things wherein there is no profit.***

I find it fascinating that it is not the Jews coming to YHVH saying they have inherited lies, but the Gentiles. This is not to say that the Jews have not inherited any lies, but the finger is quite clearly pointed at us here, so we have to accept the righteous rebuke. To combat this inheritance of lies, we must fill ourselves with the truth, from beginning to end. Everything in the Bible builds on what came before it, and it was entirely profitless when we came to faith and were told to read John and Romans – two books that were built on an intricate and deep understanding of the law and the prophets, as well as first century beliefs about the role of Messiah as taught by the ancient sages of Judaism (found in extra-biblical commentaries of the time). By stripping us of the importance of the law and the prophets, we are left flailing, trying to understand writings with no context whatsoever. No historical context, no biblical context. And *we must know that context* or people can tell us whatever they believe is true and we will not know whether or not we should believe them. And brothers and sisters – you deserve better than that. You should *study everything*, like the Berean Jews did in the book of Acts.[91] They *searched the Hebrew Scriptures (Old Testament)* in order to find out if what Paul preached was true, and were called wise. They didn't have Bibles at home, they had to unroll

---

[91] Acts 17:11

scrolls down at the synagogue, but because they did not want to be led astray towards following a false prophet, they searched and searched and came out believing.

I could be lying to you – and you have to find out.  Please, **test everything and hold to what is good.**[92]  I will not be standing beside you in the Judgment; you won't be able to point at me or your pastor and say you were just following orders.  I believe with my whole heart that what I am telling you is true, but you need to make sure.

The first rule of scriptural interpretation is that **scripture interprets scripture**.  It is not a matter of opinions, or guessing, or leaning on our own understanding.  Nothing in scripture stands by itself, and the same things are reiterated over and over again.  Words in Hebrew and Greek were carefully chosen for specific meanings, meanings that often are not faithfully reflected in English, and sometimes simply cannot be.  When the Septuagint was written (the Greek version of the Hebrew Scriptures translated a few hundred years before Yeshua), 70 rabbis carefully collaborated in order to render Hebrew into Greek as faithfully as possible, giving us a sort of "dictionary" as to what Hebrew concepts were to be conveyed by specific Greek words.  The New Testament authors were familiar with the Septuagint and used it when deciding what Greek words to use in the gospels.  Knowing this can be helpful, even for the casual biblical scholar.

One of the most important tools for studying the scriptures isn't just reading it – **we have to see what it does and does not say**.  Here are some questions:

1.  When was Yeshua born?
2.  How many Magi were at His birth?
3.  What day of the week did Messiah die?
4.  Where was Adam created?

---

[92] I Thess 5:21

Answer to question #1 – Yeshua was born in the fall and not the winter. If you recall, it snowed this last year in Israel. December is too cold for shepherds to be out with their sheep at night.[93] We assume winter because of tradition, but clues in the text that would have made perfect sense to Jews in Luke's day point to the Feast of Tabernacles in the fall. (As Luke was writing to Theophilus, the son of Caiaphas the High Priest, he would not have to explain his references at all)

Answer to question #2 – None. Some Magi showed up approximately two years later,[94] but we don't know how many Magi, we only know how many gifts. Only Shepherds were there for the royal birth.[95] We believe there were three because of tradition. No little drummer boy either – he would have been in Jerusalem for the Feast.

Answer to question #3 – This one proves you have to know the OT, because Yeshua died right before the Sabbath,[96] which on a normal week would make His death on a Friday, but during Passover week there are generally 3 Sabbaths within a seven day period! Not understanding this led to the logical conclusion that He must have died on a Friday, when in actuality He had to die on a Wednesday or Thursday in order to rise at the end of the weekly Sabbath or early Sunday morning. We believe Friday because of tradition.

Answer to question #4 – I always love to bring up this one. It really caught me off guard. I thought Adam was created in the Garden of Eden, but he wasn't, he was created on the outside and brought into the garden.[97]

This is why we must pay careful attention when reading about things we think we know because our preconceived notions and traditions will blind us to what is otherwise clearly written. Even after years of this, I

---

[93] Luke 2:8
[94] Matt 2:16
[95] Luke 2:16
[96] John 19:31
[97] Gen 2:7-8; Gen 3:23

find that I have sacred cows tipped on a regular basis – which is a very good thing and I am always joyful when I find them, even if it hurts my pride a bit.

It is our natural inclination to read our traditions and desires into the text, and learning not to do that is a lifelong process as well as an act of YHVH's mercy towards us whenever we do see what is actually there instead of what we want to be there.

Surely Jeremiah was right – we have inherited lies and we didn't even have a clue!

But don't waste time being angry about the lies, always rejoice in the truth because the truth is a gift. Indeed, no one complains about their old worn out shoes when they are given a new pair!

## But I Can't Keep 613 Laws

I have good news for you. No one ever had to do that, not even Yeshua. And now, without a standing Temple, we automatically cannot observe 58% of them – if we tried, we would actually be sinning because there are laws in place to keep us from doing what we want wherever we want.

The truth is, that a great many laws are only for Levites (descendants of the tribe of Levi) and Aaronic Priests (direct line male descendants of Aaron, Moses' brother). Many laws require a standing Temple, or at least a consecrated altar in the place YHVH chose, which currently happens to be covered with one of the most revered Muslim shrines on earth. Some laws are only for men, or women, or children. Some laws are for government, Kings, and wars. Some are for thieves – don't steal anything and it won't concern you! Some are for murderers – again, don't murder anyone and they won't apply to you.

Doug Friedman did a breakdown of the 613 laws and discovered something amazing.[98]

58% cannot be observed today
28% of the remaining 42% are currently kept by Bible Believing Christians!
6% more are kept, to varying degrees, by those who make a point to try and pursue a Torah lifestyle
8% are not kept at all (some are culturally impossible to enforce)

I want you to look carefully at that – you are probably already keeping 67% of the laws of Torah that can currently be kept. And the really tragic thing is that most of the ones that aren't being kept are the ones

---

[98] www.messianicassociation.org/ezine22-df.mosaic-laws-messianic.htm This is an amazing resource. My thanks to David Freeman for graciously allowing me to cite it and I encourage you to read through his research in context.

that involve God's celebrations, the days that YHVH set aside so we can be with Him to celebrate His prophetic pictures of what has been and what will be.  These are the very laws that provide proof that Yeshua is Messiah!  *These are the ones that are the sign we told to have on the back of our hand and on our forehead.*

### YHVH's Appointed Times

God's appointed times, in Hebrew, are called moedim. We see the first mention in Genesis 1, on the fourth day when the sun, moon and stars were created.

*1:14 And God said, Let there be lights in the firmament of the heaven to divide the day from the night; and let them be for signs, and for seasons, and for days, and years:*

The word "seasons" is an unfortunate translation of the word moed, meaning an appointment, a festival, or a set time. It does not mean winter, spring, summer and fall. On the fourth day, before He created a single living being – He set up a system so that we could celebrate with Him. Celebrations, His celebrations, are extremely important to God.

Sabbath – our weekly celebration, our day of rest, to be kept forever; looking forward to the 7th Millennium when Messiah will reign on earth.

Passover/Unleavened Bread/First Fruits – the early Spring Feasts, commemorating a release from slavery in Egypt and ordained as a prophetic picture looking forward to the Lamb of YHVH who was slain for the world, now celebrated as a memorial Feast.

Shavuot (Pentecost) – the later Spring Feast. The celebration of the giving of the ten commandments to the assembly from Mt Sinai, and a prophetic picture of the giving of the Holy Spirit to the believing assembly who were at the Temple for the first Feast of Shavuot after the resurrection, now celebrated as a memorial Feast.

Yom Teruah – the Feast of Trumpets, the first Fall Feast celebrated on the first day of Tishri as observed by the sighting of the first sliver of the new moon, it is the feast that occurs on the day and hour that no man knows, which we still celebrate as we await the fulfillment of this Feast (as we do for all the following Fall Feasts).

161

Yom Kippur – the Day of Atonement, the second Fall Feast, the holiest day of the year, when the sins of the nation are atoned for.

Sukkot – The third Fall Feast, also called the Feast of Tabernacles or the Feast of Booths.

HaShanna Rabbah – the final Fall Feast, also known as the last day of Sukkot, the Last Great Day.

These are all the days, listed in Leviticus 23, that YHVH commanded us to observe forever, the entire nation of Israel. Remember Ephesians 2? We are full citizens now of the Commonwealth of Israel, these Feasts are ours by familial rights just like the 4th of July belongs to any child adopted from a foreign country by an American family. Sadly, because of ancient Roman legislation and pressure outlawing the 7th day Sabbath and the Feasts of YHVH, a great many of our forefathers in the faith were not willing to die for their beliefs and caved to pagan persecution. Many of those who refused to compromise died for their beliefs. Although the Jews kept faithfully celebrating at all costs, the now largely former Gentile Church went back to the ways of their pagan ancestors in the second, third and fourth centuries – incorporating whatever pagan rites that were demanded of them by Rome. Perhaps in the beginning they thought that the persecution would end someday and things would go back to the way they were in the first and second centuries, but that didn't happen. What began under persecution became tradition, as normal believers had no access to their own Bible and relied completely on what the priests were telling them for over a thousand years. This also happened in ancient Israel during its own dark ages.

*Ezekiel 22:26 **Her priests have violated my law,** and have profaned mine holy things: they have **put no difference between the holy and profane,** neither have they shewed difference between **the unclean and*** *the clean, and **have hid their eyes from my sabbaths**, and **I am profaned among them**.*

Again, what has happened before happened again. But the truth is, one way or another, we were robbed of our inheritance, the days of our joy and celebration. We were stripped of our rights as believers to keep the very Feasts that were there not only to honor God, but were also there to show us Messiah. Without them we cannot perceive the times, nor can we be a light to our Jewish brothers and sisters who see our law-breaking as proof that Yeshua is not the Messiah. This heartbreaking stumbling block is barring our Jewish brothers and sisters from entering into the Kingdom of Heaven, which has always been the goal of the enemy.

What was one of the works of the deceiver supposed to be?

*Dan 7:25a And he shall speak great words against the most High, and shall wear out the saints of the most High, **and think to change times and laws***

And that was exactly the influence of the Roman rulers on the faith once delivered to the saints. They wore down the leaders and they changed the times and the laws. Some wanted to join the community of Hadrian and others simply wanted to save their own lives. But the cost has been tragic. Once stripped of its roots from Sinai, the assembly of believers lost all reckoning of time and all reverence for the laws.

Blessedly this is changing, and many of us have woken up; we are hard at work preparing to meet with our Bridegroom at His appointed times so that we can be ready when He returns to take us to the place prepared for us. We are making up for lost time!

I would love to take you through the Feasts of YHVH. Never are they called the Feasts of the Jews, but God Himself calls them by His own

Name. They are the Feasts of YHVH. They are the Appointed Festivals of our God and King, and prophetic shadows of good things to come.

### When Does the Day Begin and What is the Sabbath?

Taking the cue from Genesis 1, Jews begin and end each day at Sundown.  And so nothing starts at midnight, or when the sun comes up.

Gen 1:5, 8, 13, 19, 23, and 31 all have this statement

*And the **evening** and the morning were the (first, second, third, etc.) day.*

Leviticus Chap 15 talks about various kinds of uncleanness that would bar someone from being at the Tabernacle/Temple and in each case, the person was to wash and then they would be clean at evening, signifying a fresh start the next day.

There are many other examples, but this is really not a point of debate with the overwhelming majority of people, it just takes a bit of getting used to!  The Jews have observed the day as starting at sundown for many millennium, in recognition of God's reckoning of time.

Now that we have our days straightened out, did you know that the Jews call the weekly Sabbath "the wedding ring of the Covenant?"  They actually attribute a large part of their blessed status on this earth to their collective keeping of the Sabbath.  Say what you will, but despite their continual persecution over the millennia, they are the most blessed people on earth.  They are blessed in part because of God's promise to Abraham, but in addition, of all the people on earth, they are trying the hardest to get it right according to the Covenant delivered to their fathers.  In some things, they also have it wrong, but no one can fault them for not being zealous.  They deeply and ardently care about doing things God's way.

Did you know that for a great many years in America, believing Christians actually did observe a Sabbath rest?  In fact, they kept a great deal more of the law than modern Christians do, and they were blessed far more than we are. Although our Christian ancestors kept the wrong day because of church tradition, still they did not work, nor did they buy and sell on Sunday. I believe with all my heart that God honored that commitment and reverence.

Yes, I did mention that they kept the wrong day, and most still do. It started with pressure from Rome during the second century, which was formalized in 321 AD by the Emperor Constantine

*On the venerable Day of the sun let the magistrates and people residing in cities rest, and let all workshops be closed. In the country, however, persons engaged in agriculture may freely and lawfully continue their pursuits: because it often happens that another Day is not so suitable for grain sowing or for vine planting: lest by neglecting the proper moment for such operations the bounty of heaven should be lost.*[99]

Constantine actually commanded that formal worship be moved to Sunday from Saturday. And he wasn't shy about showing his continued devotion to the sun god he worshiped by insisting that Sunday, the day devoted to the sun god Mithras, was to be agriculturally worked on, because it was the best day for planting – a very pagan doctrine indeed! But that wasn't the worst. In 364 AD the Catholic Church Council at Laodicea (yes, lukewarm Laodicea) decreed the following:

*Christians shall not Judaize and be idle on Saturday (Sabbath), but shall work on that Day: but the Lord's Day, they shall especially honour; and as being Christians, shall, if possible, do no work on that day. If however, they are found Judaizing, they shall be shut out from Christ.*[100]

---

[99] Edward Gibbon, *The history of the decline and fall of the Roman Empire* Volume 3 (London: 1838): 237

[100] Rev. Charles Joseph Hefele, Henry N. Oxenham (trans.), *A History of the Church Councils from 326 to 429* Volume 2 (Edinburgh: T. and T. Clark, 1896): 316.

166

(Side note: Ever wonder where the word Judaizer comes from? Not from the Bible, but from the persecutors and traitors to the faith. It was a term cooked up in order to justify the expulsion and persecution of Messianic Jews from the assembly of believers. It was also utilized to ferment hatred between the Jews and later followers of Yeshua. I don't know about you, but looking for instruction in righteousness from lukewarm Laodicea just doesn't seem like a wise course of action.)

Certainly there was no need for such a decree if the apostles had kept a Sunday Sabbath, as many suggest. We must again chalk up our modern understanding to tradition, tradition that has been bolstered by verses taken out of context. And we are now told to celebrate the Sunday Sabbath because Yeshua was raised from the dead on Sunday – but why was Sabbath instituted in the first place? God's Feasts are there for a reason – and the reason for the Sabbath has always been two-fold and very specific.

The first reason is that we are celebrating Creation. When we keep the 7th day Sabbath, we are making the proclamation that God created the earth in 6 days and rested on the 7th. It is a statement of faith that the first chapter of Genesis is absolute truth. Here's the proof from Ex 20.

*8-11 Remember the sabbath day, to keep it holy. Six days shalt thou labour, and do all thy work: but the seventh day is the sabbath of the LORD thy God: in it thou shalt not do any work, thou, nor thy son, nor thy daughter, thy manservant, nor thy maidservant, nor thy cattle, nor thy stranger that is within thy gates: **For in six days the LORD made heaven and earth, the sea, and all that in them is, and rested the seventh day: wherefore the LORD blessed the sabbath day, and hallowed it.***

If we change the Sabbath day, we nullify its intent in order to make it mean what we want it to mean. John says that Yeshua, the living Word of God, created everything

*John 1:3 **All things were made by him; and without him was not any thing made that was made.***

So now the Sabbath is a double declaration, the second declaration being that Yeshua made the heavens and the earth, the sea and all that is in them and rested on the 7$^{th}$ day, that He blessed it, and hallowed it. Keeping the Sabbath then, is following and honoring Yeshua as Creator, just as He commanded.

And on an even deeper level, as we come to the end of the 6000 years of history, we are eagerly awaiting the 7$^{th}$ millennium, where Yeshua's return and give us 1000 years of peace. The 7$^{th}$ day is important; it always has been and always will be. Moving the Sabbath to the first day takes away any prophetic foreshadowing of Yeshua's coming earthly Kingdom, it strips the Sabbath of all its intended meaning.

Tradition, and an enemy changing the times and laws, robbed us of it.

If you notice, the Council of Laodicea used an interesting term that is now in common usage in the Church, the Lord's Day, but where did this term come from and what does it mean Biblically? It is found only one place in scripture:

*Rev 1:10 I was in the Spirit **on the Lord's day**, and heard behind me a great voice, as of a trumpet,*

Remember that nothing is established without two or three witnesses? Well, in order to make the Lord's Day mean Sunday, we need those witnesses. Let's do a search through scripture for the words Lord and day in the same sentence and see what we find.

I have eleven distinct witnesses who all attest to the identity of the Lord's Day, throughout scripture. For brevity, I will only include one quote from each, because some of the prophets mention it many times.

Isaiah 2:12 For **the day of the LORD** of hosts shall be upon every one that is proud and lofty, and upon every one that is lifted up; and he shall be brought low:

Jeremiah 46:10 For this is **the day of the Lord** GOD of hosts, a day of vengeance, that he may avenge him of his adversaries: and the sword shall devour, and it shall be satiate and made drunk with their blood: for the Lord GOD of hosts hath a sacrifice in the north country by the river Euphrates.

Ezekiel 7:19 They shall cast their silver in the streets, and their gold shall be removed: their silver and their gold shall not be able to deliver them in **the day of the wrath of the LORD**: they shall not satisfy their souls, neither fill their bowels: because it is the stumbling block of their iniquity.

Joel 1:15 Alas for the day! for **the day of the LORD** is at hand, and as a destruction from the Almighty shall it come.

Amos 5:18 Woe unto you that desire **the day of the LORD**! to what end is it for you? the day of the LORD is darkness, and not light.

Obadiah 1:15 For **the day of the LORD** is near upon all the heathen: as thou hast done, it shall be done unto thee: thy reward shall return upon thine own head.

Zephaniah 1:14-15 **The great day of the LORD** is near, it is near, and hasteth greatly, even the voice of the day of the LORD: the mighty man shall cry there bitterly. That day is a day of wrath, a day of trouble and distress, a day of wasteness and desolation, a day of darkness and gloominess, a day of clouds and thick darkness,

Zechariah 14:1 Behold, **the day of the LORD** cometh, and thy spoil shall be divided in the midst of thee.

*Malachi 4:5 Behold, I will send you Elijah the prophet before the coming of the great and dreadful* **day of the LORD**

*Paul – I Thess 5:2 For yourselves know perfectly that* **the day of the Lord** *so cometh as a thief in the night.*

*Peter – 2 Peter 3:10 But* **the day of the Lord** *will come as a thief in the night; in the which the heavens shall pass away with a great noise, and the elements shall melt with fervent heat, the earth also and the works that are therein shall be burned up.*

These eleven prophets and apostles all clearly establish that the Day of the Lord is the time spoken of throughout the Book of Revelation. So now let us look once more at what John was saying, in context.

*Rev 1:10 I was in the Spirit* **on the Day of the LORD**, *and heard behind me a great voice, as of a trumpet (changes mine)*

John was in the Spirit, having a revelatory vision, not on Sunday (although it might have been on a Sunday, we have no idea, there's a one in seven chance), but in order to detail the revelation of the Day of the Lord to the assemblies of God. The Lord's day being Sunday is founded only in tradition, resulting from the persecution of the early followers of Yeshua. Sabbath will never change, indeed it cannot.

We will even keep the Sabbath during the Millennium Kingdom.

*Isaiah 66:23 And it shall come to pass, that from one new moon to another, and* **from one sabbath to another,** *shall all flesh come to worship before me, saith the LORD.*

You might ask, "Well then, how do we celebrate the resurrection?" I am so glad you asked, because YHVH thought of everything, and I am going to introduce you to the day of First Fruits later on when we talk about the Spring Feasts.

## Our Two Weeks of Unrest

Before I go into the Feasts of YHVH, I am going to tell you about the week we broke the Sabbath. I guess I could also call it the terrible, horrible, no good, very bad two weeks.

We had been dutifully resting on the Sabbath for 2 ½ years, and we really never had to be forced to obey that one. After all, napping is my favorite pastime! I also love reading the Scriptures and talking about it with my husband, watching internet teachings together and learning new things.

But then came the weekend where Mark, my husband, got worried about the stability of His job. He had a friend from long back coming in from Idaho to do some consultant work and Mark didn't have to be there, but we decided that since he is on salary and wasn't getting paid, and wasn't really working, it would be okay. He even brought his Bible to read in his office while he was supervising the work. See how holy we tried to make it look to ourselves?

Well, I wasn't at work, but I felt awful all day – something was wrong. I was tired, and not feeling restful at all. I started wishing that Mark would come home. It wasn't Sabbath without him. No one in the family felt right. And the next day? Mark and I both felt like we had been hit with a Mack Truck and that feeling of tiredness lingered for two whole weeks. We were short tempered, and just everything was off. We knew right away we had done wrong, that we were (pardon the expression) guilty as sin. We knew better. And our Heavenly Father was making sure we knew we had better never do it again. Mark broke it in action; I broke it through my approval.

Mark and I both agreed that to live like that permanently would be tantamount to hell on earth, so we aren't going to do that again. I'd rather have him get fired, honestly, and trust God to provide for us. But that is His love, giving us the consequences and the opportunity to repent. We got grounded for breaking the rules of the house.

On another level, I am also grateful for the lesson because sometimes we get lukewarm about the commandments, and when we have started to enjoy the blessings for obedience, we forget that our lives used to be a lot harder. I need the Sabbath rest, it is a gift from YHVH, and because we broke it once on purpose, now I can tell everyone the consequences for disobedience and the benefits of obedience.

It's a win-win situation. In fact, all of the failures in our walk can be profitable if we learn from them and teach what we learned to others.

And now on to the rest of the Feasts, but before I do, I want to combat a piece of social conditioning against God's laws that you may be totally unaware of, and that you probably even approve of, because I sure did; I hope I can change that.

## Animal Sacrifice

The biggest theological objection to animal sacrifice is that Yeshua was the last sacrifice, and for sin as well as atonement that is partially true (give me a bit of your time and I will clarify). However, the overwhelming majority of sacrifices had nothing to do with sin at all! There were memorial offerings on Feast days, thanksgiving offerings, and some offerings were actually flour, oil, frankincense and salt burned on the altar.[101] The offerings were a way of saying, "Here is this valuable thing, it is Yours, please accept it." And the fragrance of the animal roasting on the altar would go up to YHVH for a pleasing aroma.[102] Sometimes, part of the animal would be eaten by those giving it, in His presence, and sometimes part of it would go to the priests to feed them, but in an agrarian society, the giving of an animal was like burning money. It was something offered to God and only to God; it was an act of love and a way of showing Him honor publicly, of drawing near to Him.

But our modern minds have been trained to hate this one. We think of suffering animals being lined up, blood gushing out everywhere, priests soaked in blood, the sound of terrified bleats and mooing – but it wasn't like that at all. In fact, you will probably be shocked to hear that it was a very peaceful situation. We know from Jewish writings that the animal to be sacrificed had to be completely calm before having its throat cut with a knife so razor sharp that the process was done quickly.

But people still think this is barbaric – people who have no qualms about eating meat from the supermarket. Well, those animals are slaughtered too.

---

[101] Lev 2 details this type of offering
[102] Lev 1:9

Like many of the things we have encountered in this book, what we are largely dealing with is social conditioning and preconceived notions that are not rooted in fact. Modern western peoples have been trained by animal rights groups not just to respect the basic dignity of animals, but to actually, in many cases, care for them more than humans. Am I the only person who knows someone who protects a biting dog at all costs, who will lie to protect them, even at the expense of the humans who are in danger? I grew up in a neighborhood where a dog practically tore the throat out of a first grader in the street in front of their house. Yes she lived, but the owners were infuriated when they had to lock up their dog afterwards! If it were me, the dog would be dead, no matter how much I loved it, even if I had to do it myself. Humans come before animals, period.

In general, the people who hate animal cruelty have no problem with stepping on insects – the bigger the better. But do insects feel pain and fear less acutely than cute, furry animals?

We pass around quotes about how a society can be judged by how it treats its animals and to a degree, it is true – no society should be needlessly cruel. But we need, as in all things – as I have tried to communicate throughout this book – to see this situation through God's eyes and not our own. We need to realize that if anyone's ideas are warped, well, they aren't His! Can I get agreement on that? His ideas of right and wrong, good and bad, appropriate and inappropriate are perfect. It's our minds that need to be conformed to His.

I read a disturbing blog this morning by a Christian, who said that animal sacrifices were an imperfect solution made by an **imperfect god** (I put a little g on that one because I just couldn't put the word imperfect in front of a "big G" god). Whoa there – blasphemy alert. I hope that I have already proven beyond a shadow of a doubt that that cannot be true. What I will say is that sin sacrifices were a temporary act of faith, pointing to the perfect solution, made by a perfect God. The sin sacrifices were perfect in that they pointed perfectly towards the coming Messiah, but imperfect in that each animal could only cover for the transgressions that came before it, not those which came after it. Whenever our repentance is true, the blood of Yeshua covers our sins once more, the perfect offering – not human sacrifice, not even a sacrifice at all because it did not meet any of the legal requirements, but the perfect freewill offering for reconciliation. Yeshua was not a sacrifice. He was not killed on the altar by the priests, in the Temple. I know this goes against what we were taught, but I encourage you to study for yourself. Yeshua did not take the place of an animal on the cross – He took our place.

All sin offerings were freewill – no one was ever forced to do it. This was the same for all voluntary offerings. They brought offerings out of love and respect and devotion, not because they thought they were serving a bloodthirsty deity.

There were, in fact, offerings that had nothing to do with blood at all – grains were often offered, with the same response from YHVH – they were a pleasing aroma to Him. This is one we can probably all agree on, the smell of fresh baked bread is glorious!

I hope this helps clarify it, even though I have barely scratched the surface here. In all things, when we struggle, it helps to ask our Heavenly Father to help us see things as He does. We do not want to find ourselves thinking uncharitable, humanistic, worldy-inspired thoughts about Him.

## The Spring Feasts Pt 1 – Passover

I love the movie *The Ten Commandments* with Charlton Heston. Among other things, it details both the original Passover and Shavuot. Imagine the raw power and authority of our God on display for Egypt to see, I daresay we can't even begin to imagine what it was like! People from all over the known world would have been talking about it.

The Passover was the second Feast instituted by YHVH, the yearly commemoration of the deliverance of the children of Israel from slavery in Egypt. It was also a prophetic foreshadowing of the Messiah who would be slain, on the Passover, over 1400 years later in order to reconcile us to right standing with God. As I write this, my family has begun making the preparations for the Feast and it is an exciting time. Although we do not keep it as the Jews do, with their beautiful traditions, we do observe the biblical commandments that surround the Feast.

Please keep this in mind as you look through the Feasts in the Bible – the overwhelming majority of what the Jews observe is found in the books of commentary by the sages, most notably the Talmud. Like Christian commentary, some is obviously inspired and in my opinion some is definitely not. Studying how the Jews do things provides remarkable insight to our Messiah, even though many do not see the connections. But according to Torah, these things are not required and so please do not pressure yourself to do things in a "Jewish way" if you were not brought up that way. Learn what the Bible tells you to do and if you later feel led, add some of their traditions – it really is up to you. As for our family, we still have not added any of the Jewish traditions as we are approaching our third Passover. Learning to keep the commandments can take years, so in all things treat yourself like you would treat a little child learning the rules. Please do not try advanced calculus if you cannot add and subtract – you will only set yourself up for disappointment and failure, and you will not take joy in your walk. Worst of all, sticking with the metaphor, you might walk away assuming you can't do math at all when in reality you just didn't prepare for the complicated by mastering the simple. In all things, extend grace to yourself and give yourself time to learn. Enjoy the journey!

What does the Bible say about the Feast of Passover?

*Lev 23:5 In the fourteenth day of the first month at even is the LORD's passover.*

According to the Biblical Calendar, the year begins in the Spring, when the barley is ripe. On the sighting of the first sliver of the new moon near the time of the barley harvest, we begin the year. On the fourteenth day, we celebrate the Passover Feast.

*Ex 12:42-43 It is a night to be much observed unto the LORD for bringing them out from the land of Egypt: **this is that night of the LORD to be observed of all the children of Israel in their generations**. And the LORD said unto Moses and Aaron, This is the ordinance of the passover: There shall no stranger eat thereof:*

As I have previously established, all who are in Covenant with YHVH through the blood of Yeshua are citizens of Israel and therefore the children of Israel (both native born and adopted), not strangers to the Covenants. And indeed, there is only one exclusion in the whole of Torah – if you are a male and not circumcised, you may not eat of the Passover. Passover is the one Feast that requires a whole heart commitment – just like accepting the blood of Yeshua requires a whole heart commitment and is serious business. The stranger does not work on the two High Sabbaths of the Feast and may celebrate with the Nation, but of the meal he shall not eat.

*Ex 12:48 And when a stranger shall sojourn with thee, and will keep the passover to the LORD, **let all his males be circumcised, and then let*** *him come near and keep it; and he shall be as one that is born in the land: for no uncircumcised person shall eat thereof.*

When a person desires in their heart to eat of the Passover, they must make the commitment and become circumcised; it is their choice, no one is forcing them.  Once they are circumcised, they are as one born in the Land.  As we saw in the first century, the Pharisees from the House of Shammai had used this verse to say that circumcision was required to be a part of the people of Israel, but all it really says is that in order to eat of this one meal one must be circumcised.  That is a big difference.

There is a debate now as to whether this currently applies because the lamb we eat on the night of the Passover is no longer sacrificed and therefore not a Passover lamb, but I prefer to err on the side of caution.  When we have guests over, I require that their males be circumcised.  During the feast week and throughout the year, uncircumcised men are welcome to eat with us, but on that night, we do draw the line.  It's very debatable; everyone has to make their own call on it.  I don't judge anyone who decides differently.

Can we sacrifice an animal for Passover now?  No, the commandments expressly forbid it.

*Deut 16:2, 5 Thou shalt therefore sacrifice the passover unto the LORD thy God, of the flock and the herd, **in the place which the LORD shall choose to place his name there…. Thou mayest not sacrifice the passover within any of thy gates**, which the LORD thy God giveth thee: **But at the place which the LORD thy God shall choose to place his name in**, there thou shalt sacrifice the Passover at even, at the going down of the sun, at the season that thou camest forth out of Egypt.*

Like any of the thanksgiving and peace offerings, the remembrance offerings cannot lawfully be given outside of the place where YHVH has eternally put His Name, in Jerusalem at the Temple Mount. I would, for one, love to bring a grain offering, mixed with oil and frankincense and salt, to be offered up as a pleasing aroma for YHVH at His altar. I would love it, but that doesn't matter because I do not have the right to approach YHVH according to my whims. I must honor Him by doing according to His commands.

When we keep the Passover, we are fulfilling a commandment to memorialize not only the passing over of the Children of Israel by the Angel of death, but we are also declaring our belief that Yeshua is our Passover. Everything about Passover points to the Messiah, the redeemer of Israel, who struck a death blow against the enemy who had us in slavery to sin and forced him to let us go. I love declaring that by holding a feast in His honor. He deserves it!

What did Yeshua say at His last meal before the Passover?

*Luke 22:19 And he took bread, and gave thanks, and brake it, and gave unto them, saying, This is my body which is given for you: this do in remembrance of me.*

Notice He did not say "Never keep the Passover again," but instead, from now on, "Do this in remembrance of me." He was proclaiming that tomorrow, He would be the Passover lamb.

I agree, and in my house Passover is a time of joy. We are free from the bondage of having to serve sin, and free to serve God.

Some people think that celebrating the Passover is wrong because they mistakenly believe that the animal sacrifice at Passover was a sin sacrifice, but it wasn't – it was a memorial offering, an act of thanksgiving – it was a pointing back to that first lamb in Egypt and a pointing forward to the Lamb of God. And now, it is a pointing back in gratitude and recognition of Messiah ben Joseph, the suffering servant who takes away the sins of the world.

Passover is pretty straightforward, and unlike all but one of the other days we will discuss, it is not a High Sabbath, so we can go to work that day and celebrate at night, but now we go to the real Feast that starts the next day – the Feast of Unleavened Bread, our first and second High Sabbaths of the year.

## The Spring Feasts Pt 2 – Unleavened Bread

This feast starts at sundown after the Passover, at the start of the 15<sup>th</sup> day of the first Biblical month.

*Ex 13:6-10 Seven days thou shalt eat unleavened bread, and in the seventh day shall be a feast to the LORD. Unleavened bread shall be eaten seven days; and there shall no leavened bread be seen with thee, neither shall there be leaven seen with thee in all thy quarters. And thou shalt shew thy son in that day, saying, This is done because of that which the LORD did unto me when I came forth out of Egypt. **And it shall be for a sign unto thee upon thine hand, and for a memorial between thine eyes**, that the LORD's law may be in thy mouth: for with a strong hand hath the LORD brought thee out of Egypt. Thou shalt therefore keep this ordinance in his season from year to year.*

See that bold text?  Remember I talked about the Sign of God vs the Mark of the Beast? Here's the first reference.  It directly ties to the celebration of this seven day Feast, a feast that Yeshua directly references in a teaching – if you know what to look for.

*Matt 16:6, 12 - Then Jesus said unto them, Take heed and beware of the leaven of the Pharisees and of the Sadducees. Then understood they how that he bade them not beware of the leaven of bread, but of the doctrine of the Pharisees and of the Sadducees.*

We have already looked at some of the doctrines of the Pharisees, but not at the Sadducees.  Although we see a great many Pharisees coming to faith in Yeshua after Shavuot (Pentecost) we see no mention of Sadducees coming to faith.  Why is that?  It is because they did not believe in the resurrection from the dead and the Pharisees did!  To them, it was impossible and so they could not and did not overcome their doctrinal prejudice.  As a result, they died in their unbelief.  In addition, they believed in a very shallow reading of the Bible, whereas we know the Yeshua had to "open up" the scriptures after His resurrection to show His followers how it spoke of Him. Pharisees read the Bible at a deep level in Yeshua's day, as the Orthodox still do today. Some of the writings of their great sages are astounding and point directly to Yeshua as Messiah, but many eyes are still blinded – in part by over 1800 years of persecution at the hands of those who claim to follow Jesus Christ. They hate the man that their families were persecuted in the name of, and cannot see their own Messiah. We should never point our finger at the unbelieving Jews without seeing the three fingers pointing back at Christianity. Our generations taught their generations to hate and fear their Messiah.

In Yeshua's words, leaven is related to false teachings. Indeed leaven is equivalent to anything in our lives that puffs us up and causes death – because that is what leaven does.

Leaven is the fermentation of grain, something we find in most bread products. Back in the days of the Exodus, they did not have a jar of yeast in their fridge to use – they had to ferment their bread, just as sourdough manufacturers do today, using a small lump of already fermented "starter" to leaven the next batch. Because they left so quickly, there was no time to do this and so they ate no leavened bread in the exodus out of Egypt. Therefore, when we eat unleavened bread for a week, when we remove all leaven from our homes and property, it is a proclamation that we believe the Exodus happened exactly as described and so we are celebrating our deliverance from Egypt (sin).

At a deeper spiritual level, as Yeshua taught His disciples, ridding our homes of leaven represents getting rid of the false teachings that we have lived with. The Israelites coming out of Egypt had been subject to all sorts of abominations, had lived in the midst of them, and had probably participated in them (400 years is a long time, and they didn't come up with the idea of the golden calf out of nowhere). Each year, really every day, we should make a practice of making sure that what we believe is actually the truth, and we should not be clinging to the false, no matter how good and nostalgic it makes us feel. This is a difficult process and takes time – really, it takes a lifetime.

In the week before the Passover, we search our homes for all the yeast containing products (I actually start about a month ahead of time), and we get them eaten up so as to not waste food. The important thing is that we get them identified and put somewhere where we won't forget to throw out whatever remains.

Reality check: I have not yet gotten it all. I often find something in the midst of the week or the next week that was hidden. When you have kids, things get shoved into places they aren't supposed to be. It happens. I am certainly not the only person to find a half-eaten sandwich under a couch, or to find something leavened hiding in plain sight that I just didn't see. Toss it out and ask for forgiveness, it was unintentional, and He knows it. But He loves our obedience when we figure out that we fell short of perfection and make it right – just like we love it when our kids do it.

Exodus 13:6-10 doesn't mention it, but the first and seventh days of Unleavened Bread are referred to as High Sabbaths.[103] They are different from normal Sabbaths, as we can cook, but we do no servile work (note: taking care of people's basic needs is not work, unless you are getting paid for it).

This is the day referred to in John 19:31

*The Jews therefore, because it was the preparation, that the bodies should not remain upon the cross on the sabbath day, (for **that sabbath day was an high day**,) besought Pilate that their legs might be broken, and that they might be taken away.*

---

[103] Lev 23:7-8

For a great many years, because the church has not kept the Feasts, this verse was thought to be talking about Friday – that Yeshua was crucified on Friday, but this verse is talking about the next day being the High Sabbath of the first day of the Feast of Unleavened Bread, which on that year fell on a Thursday, making Passover on a Wednesday. Believing it was a Friday has led to Christianity being mocked by the world for not knowing how to count to three – three days, three nights in the earth – with Messiah rising at the cusp between the Sabbath and the Feast of First Fruits, our next Feast Day.

When we celebrate Unleavened Bread, we are acknowledging that Yeshua released us from having to follow man-made doctrines, the leaven that puffs us up, and made us free to follow God's laws, which are much simpler and for our benefit.

You were probably wondering how to celebrate the Resurrection if not on Sunday? Good news, God thought of everything.

## The Spring Feasts Pt 3 - First Fruits

*Lev 23:10-11 Speak unto the children of Israel, and say unto them, When ye be come into the land which I give unto you, and shall reap the harvest thereof, then ye shall bring a sheaf of the firstfruits of your harvest unto the priest: And he shall wave the sheaf before the LORD, to be accepted for you:* **on the morrow after the sabbath the priest shall wave it.**

"The morrow after the Sabbath" doesn't always happen on the third day of the Feast of Unleavened Bread, but it does always happen on a Sunday because it occurs on the first day after the regular weekly Sabbath. On the year Messiah died and rose however, it did happen on the third day. Even today in Israel, there are people who gather ripe barley to present as a wave offering before YHVH. We have no temple, and so this cannot be done correctly, but they are practicing in anticipation of being able to do it appropriately in the future.

Yeshua referred to this Feast when He spoke to Mary Magdalene after the Resurrection

*John 20:17 Jesus saith unto her, Touch me not; for I am not yet ascended to my Father: but go to my brethren, and say unto them,* **I ascend unto my Father**, *and your Father; and to my God, and your God.*

Yeshua, being resurrected, was going before the Father to present Himself as the First Fruits offering from the dead as High Priest in the heavenly Temple – as at His trial, the old High Priest had invalidated his priesthood by tearing his clothing[104] in violation of Lev 21:10. In fact, it is my belief that all of the Passover memorial offerings he presided over were invalid that year. The only acceptable lamb from that day on was going to be the Lamb of God. Yeshua was not eligible to be a priest on earth, being from the tribe of Judah and not Levi, but the resurrected Yeshua was free to be a priest forever, in the order of Melchizedek, which is why He was able to present the first fruits from the dead.

---

[104] Matt 26:65; Mark 14:63

On this day, Yeshua is recognized as the first to resurrect to eternal life (as Lazarus and others simply rose to a normal life again).  This day is not a Sabbath.

## The Spring Feasts Pt 4 – Shavuot

If you go to church, you probably already celebrate this High Sabbath, single day Feast. And again, a High Sabbath is a Sabbath where cooking is permissible. It is also called the Feast of Weeks, because we count 7 weekly Sabbaths to get to it.

*Lev 23:15-16 And ye shall count unto you from the morrow after the sabbath, from the day that ye brought the sheaf of the wave offering; seven sabbaths shall be complete: Even unto the morrow after the seventh sabbath shall ye number fifty days; and ye shall offer a new meat offering unto the* Lord.

This counting process of 50 days begins on the Feast of First Fruits; the terminal day is called Shavuot, meaning weeks, and in Greek it is called Pentecost. This day is a memorial of the giving of the commandments to the assembly at Sinai, the creation of the ekklesia, the church[105] and was pointing forward to the Holy Spirit being given at the Shavuot which occurred ten days after Yeshua finally ascended to the Father as recorded in Acts chapter 1. Shavuot was one of the three "pilgrimage feasts" where all the native born males living in the Land were required to go to Jerusalem and celebrate, the other two being Passover and Sukkot.[106] Why were women not required to attend? Women were welcome, but certainly a pregnant woman would not be up for the journey, and because ritual cleanliness was required to go to the Temple, a woman having her period was excused. In addition, having to drag a bunch of little ones to Jerusalem and back was no great fun, I am certain. YHVH made a solemn promise to His people that if they went, their lands and remaining family would be safe and that promise was never broken.[107]

In the verse I provided, you see that a non-sin sacrifice was given to honor YHVH. There were also grain offerings.

---

[105] Acts 7:38
[106] Ex 23:17; Deut 16:16
[107] Ex 34:24

When we celebrate Shavuot, we are thanking YHVH for the gifts of His Covenant laws and for the gift of His Holy Spirit, tying the two together! Certainly something worth celebrating!

## The Fall Feasts Pt 1 – Yom Teruah

The Biblical 7<sup>th</sup> month, the month of Tishri, is the happiest time of year for those who pursue a whole bible lifestyle.  It is an entire month focused on YHVH, where we look back to Yeshua's atonement for us with repentant hearts and look forward to His future fulfillment of the Feasts when He returns.  This is a joyous time for Jews, but for followers of Yeshua, it is a thrilling time as we await the coming of the Bridegroom, the King of Kings who will rule and reign for 1000 years here on earth.

During those days, we cry "Bo Yeshua,"  "Come salvation."  Come Messiah!

*Matt 24:36 But of that day and hour knoweth no man, no, not the angels of heaven, but my Father only.*

This verse makes little to no sense when taught out of context – it has become the clarion call of pre-tribulation rapturists who claim that Yeshua could return at any moment but once we know the Feasts and recognize that nothing about Yeshua's past, present or future ministry, was even remotely random, we see that this prophecy is tied to the very first of the Fall Feasts – the Feast of Trumpets.

*Lev 23:24-25 Speak unto the children of Israel, saying, In the seventh month, in the first day of the month, shall ye have a sabbath, a memorial of blowing of trumpets, an holy convocation.*

*Ye shall do no servile work therein: but ye shall offer an offering made by fire unto the LORD.*

In some ways, this is the absolutely most exciting day on the Biblical Calendar, as it is the day many expect Yeshua to return and gather His people, right before pouring out the final wrath on the Beast and those who have joined with him.  We know, from studying scriptures, that even now, many terrible things must happen before that day, but on

Yom Teruah, we celebrate our future deliverance from the ruler of this world. It is a joyous day!

I want to explain about trumpets in scripture, or shofar. Now there are silver trumpets (chatsotserah) that only the priests blow,[108] but there is also the shofar (a "trumpet" made of the horn of a clean animal), which anyone could blow. The teruah, translated in verse 25 as the blowing of a trumpet, is the actual sound of the shofar. Unfortunately, like the word "law" in NT Greek, translations into English have not differentiated between them. The silver trumpets were blown by the priests on certain holy days, but anyone could blow a shofar. What both the shofar and the trumpets have in common is that they were never blown for the sake of unbelievers, but for the sake of believers – so whenever you see the blowing of a trumpet, think, "Wake up Israel (that's us and the entire nation of believers), and pay attention, something is up." When you read the Book of Revelation, keep that in mind. The trumpets are not being blown for the world, but for us.

Why is it known as the Feast which occurs on the day and hour which no man knows? It is because we are never quite sure exactly when it will happen. We know the season, we know the week, we even know the three day time frame, but we do not know the exact day or hour.

Let me explain.

During Yeshua's day, Jewish writings tell us that the new months were determined by the sighting of the first sliver of the new moon. Two separate witnesses had to see it (there's those two witnesses again!), and they would hurry up to the Temple to tell the priests what they saw. The priest would then officially declare the beginning of the month and the shofar would be blown – and in the 7th month, that meant the beginning of a High Sabbath, the Feast of Trumpets. The mountain signal fires would be lit and soon all of Israel would know that the Feast had commenced.

---

[108] Num 10:2

Side note – ever wonder why the 9<sup>th</sup>, 10<sup>th</sup>, 11<sup>th</sup> and 12<sup>th</sup> month of the calendar year start with sept, oct, no, and dec? It's okay, it never occurred to me either. Septa = 7, Octo = 8, Nona = 9 and Deca = 10 in Latin. Why are the calendar names two months off?

It is a remaining witness of the calendar as it was before we took on the Roman calendar we have today. The months we know today, as well as the days of the week, are named after angels, pagan gods and roman emperors – except those 4, hearkening back to a time when the months were numbered, and determined by the moon and sun, instead of set and calculated. I find it fascinating that even though we have been forced to run our modern lives by a pagan calendar, it still bears witness to God's calendar

Tishri begins either in September or early October. It all depends on the phase of the moon! And once every few years we tack on an extra month, to make sure that the barley will be ripe for Passover, like we did this year. The Muslim calendar, by contrast, uses the moon (as their god is the moon god) but never adds a corrective month; this is why Ramadan gets earlier every single year. But in Genesis 1:14, it is written that both of the great lights in the heavens were given for the reckoning of seasons (mo'ed or feasts), days (the beginning and end of each) and years (the determining of the beginning by both lunar phase, the sign in the sky shown to Aaron and Moses by YHVH, as adjusted by the sun so that the barley crop will be ready).

Back to the Feast – we celebrate this in remembrance not only of the trumpets from Heaven at Sinai, but also as a statement of faith that Yeshua will return on the day and hour which no man knows!

Aren't Feasts as declarations of faith thrilling? Do you see how they please YHVH because they are an act of worship and proclamations of His truth? No wonder He says to celebrate forever. He wants us to (1) never forget and (2) always be declaring His promises in our thoughts, words and actions – teaching them to our generations through yearly rehearsals.

Next, we travel forward nine days to the holiest day of the year, and see Yeshua's partial fulfillment of it.

### The Fall Feasts Pt 2 – Yom Kippur

*Lev 23:27-32 Also on the tenth day of this seventh month there shall be a day of atonement: it shall be an holy convocation unto you; and **ye shall afflict your souls**, and offer an offering made by fire unto the* Lord. *And **ye shall do no work in that same day**: for it is a day of atonement, to make an atonement for you before the* Lord *your God. For whatsoever soul it be that shall not be afflicted in that same day, he shall be cut off from among his people.*

*And whatsoever soul it be that doeth any work in that same day, the same soul will I destroy from among his people. Ye shall do no manner of work: **it shall be a statute for ever** throughout your generations in all your dwellings. It shall be unto you a sabbath of rest, and ye shall afflict your souls: in the ninth day of the month at even, from even unto even**, shall ye celebrate** your sabbath.*

Yom Kippur is a Feast like none other; it is the Day of Atonement, of coverings. Unlike Passover, which represents a personal salvation from the slavery of sin, Yom Kippur is about national deliverance. We don't do our hair, or put on our makeup, we don't brush our teeth – nor do we drink water or eat anything for 24 hours. It is symbolic of our personal repentance for our sins against YHVH over the past year, collectively as the commonwealth of Israel, the nation of believers in Covenant. Can you imagine if, one day a year, every single believer in Yeshua as Messiah humbled themselves in prayer and repentance before God? We would have no need of scheduling any "National Day of Prayer" because God already instituted it 3500 years ago.

It is a day of circumcising our flesh and a day where pride has no place.

In the times before the loss of the Ark of the Covenant during the Babylonian destruction of Jerusalem, besides the sacrifice of a bull specifically for the sins of the priest, two goats, perfect ones, would be chosen and lots would be drawn.[109] One was sacrificed to YHVH and the

---

[109] Lev 16 details the Yom Kippur sacrifices

sins of the nation would be placed on the other, the "scapegoat" – which was sent out into the wilderness. Thus YHVH would cover the sins of the entire nation for another year. This scapegoat, of course, also pointed the way for One who would cover the Nation once and for all.

During the time of Yeshua, the ark was gone, and the blood of the sacrifice could no longer be placed on the Ark of the Covenant. So they came up with another idea, they would hang a red ribbon in the city, and miraculously, the Jerusalem Talmud (an earlier version of the Talmud, dated roughly at the end of the 4th century) and the Babylonian Talmud (what is normally simply referred to as "The Talmud" which we have discussed previously) both record that the ribbon would turn white each year UNTIL the year Yeshua died, 40 years before the destruction of the Temple, and then it never turned white again.

*"Our rabbis taught: During the last forty years before the destruction of the Temple the lot ['For the Lord'] did not come up in the right hand; nor did the crimson-colored strap become white; nor did the western most light shine; and the doors of the Hekel [Temple] would open by themselves"*[110]

This must have been terrifying for the nation. And indeed the first time it happened they were alarmed but probably thought it was a fluke, but year after year until the destruction of the Temple, they kept trying and kept failing to provoke a miraculous sign that they were indeed covered. From the day of Yeshua's death, the only way to achieve personal or national atonement was through the renewed Covenant in His blood, so the sacrifice was fulfilled – but not our need for corporate repentance, which is why the law says to keep it forever. Repentance is something that should never go out of style.

Again, this is a High Sabbath, and we are to celebrate it – not with a party, but with grateful repentance because Yeshua became our scapegoat, the innocent party that the blame for our sins was taken

---

[110] Babylonian Talmud, Soncino version, Yoma 39b

upon. It is a humbling thing to think on, the price He paid to cover us perfectly. It is now a statement of faith that Yeshua is our atonement once and for all.

But there is also a future fulfillment of this coming, when Yeshua does battle with the armies of the earth, the final battle with those not covered by His blood.

## The Fall Feasts Pt 3 – Sukkot

*Lev 23:34-36 Speak unto the children of Israel, saying, The fifteenth day of this seventh month shall be the feast of tabernacles for seven days unto the LORD. On the first day shall be an holy convocation: ye shall do no servile work therein. Seven days ye shall offer an offering made by fire unto the LORD: on the eighth day shall be an holy convocation unto you; and ye shall offer an offering made by fire unto the LORD: it is a solemn assembly; and ye shall do no servile work therein.*

Now, there is a raging debate about Sukkot vs Yom Teruah being the actual birthdate of Yeshua, but scholars pretty much all agree it was one or the other, and both sides have really good arguments. I am not going to say I am correct, but I will present this as though I am, because what else can I do? This walk in our Father's instructions is about doing the best we can with the information we have until we have better information. So I invoke my childhood privileges (as a Child of God) and say I may be off in this. I encourage you to do your own research into this most wonderful birth and make up your own mind.

Two Feasts are recorded in these verses, but here I will only cover Sukkot, also referred to as the Feast of Tabernacles or the Feast of Booths. This Feast recognizes the days in the wilderness, living in tents, where YHVH cared for the Nation after the Exodus. In my opinion, it has already seen a partial fulfillment in the birth of Yeshua.

*John 1:14 And the Word was made flesh, and dwelt among us, (and we beheld his glory, the glory as of the only begotten of the Father,) full of grace and truth.*

Now I have a bone to pick with the translators, but I recognize that they were unavoidably oblivious to the importance of the Feasts (these were, after all, men who were just as influenced by tradition as we are, and far removed from the context of Biblical times and culture) and so they changed skenoo, a word that means a definite thing (to encamp or to tent), from the root word skenos (a hut or temporary dwelling) and really weakened it and stripped it of any Biblical ties to the rest of the Word.  So let's change the verse to reflect this word skenoo.

*John 1:14 And the Word was made flesh, and encamped in a temporary dwelling among us, (and we beheld his glory, the glory as of the only begotten of the Father,) full of grace and truth* (revision mine)

Well, looking at that I would say that that is exactly what the Feast of Tabernacles is talking about, living in temporary dwellings away from where they have come from and where they are going to.  In Yeshua's case it represented the exchange of an immortal body for a mortal one, only to take up immortality once more.

*Lev 23:42-43 **Ye shall dwell in booths seven days**; all that are Israelites born shall dwell in booths:*

*That your generations may know that I made the children of Israel to dwell in booths, when I brought them out of the land of Egypt: I am the LORD your God.*

Wow!  This was a unique feast, a feast where the nation of Israel dwelled in tents, first wherever the Tabernacle was and then in the city of Jerusalem.

And why were there no rooms in town when Yeshua was born?  Simply put, because every man in Bethlehem would have been in Jerusalem for the Feast, whereas Mary went into labor and they were forced to set up the Sukkah (temporary dwelling) they had brought to live in during the Feast, just a few miles away in Bethlehem.  Yeshua wasn't laying in an animal feeder, but in a Sukkah.  The shepherds were on the lookout for a temporary dwelling, which would have been more obvious than checking all the buildings and caves in Bethlehem.

Now someone might object that this means Joseph was breaking Torah law in not being in Jerusalem for the Feast as commanded.  But remember, according to Yeshua and supported by the Pharisees, loving one's neighbor is the higher law and leaving Mary alone while she was giving birth would have amounted to a very grave sin indeed.

I hope I have established that every Feast is there to memorialize something and to point ahead to something even greater. As Paul said, "they are shadows of good things to come,"[111] and therefore must be kept or we will forget, as we did indeed forget for about 1800 years. And as Paul said in the verse before it, don't let anyone judge you for keeping them either – not for keeping them, or how you keep them, except the Body of Messiah.[112] The Feasts are not only commandments, but divine gifts so that we will not be ignorant of the times. YHVH does not want us in the dark as the world is in the dark.

*I Thess 5:1-6 But of the **times and the seasons*** (remember that in the Hebrew, seasons are moedim, the divine appointments from Gen 1:14) *brethren, ye have no need that I write unto you.*

*For yourselves know perfectly that **the day of the Lord** so cometh as a thief in the night.*

*For when **they*** (not the people who know the times and seasons) *shall say, Peace and safety; then sudden destruction cometh upon them, as travail upon a woman with child; and they shall not escape.*

*But **ye, brethren, are not in darkness**,* (because they knew the times and moedim) *that that day should overtake you as a thief.*

*Ye are all the children of light, and the children of the day: we are not of the night, nor of darkness.*

---

[111] Col 2:17

[112] Col 2:16-17 – note that an unnecessary "is" is added to verse 17, it should read "but the body of Christ." So we are to let no (pagan) man judge us ... (about the things we do that are commanded by God).... but the body of Christ. Only fellow believers have the right to judge us, and if we are keeping the commandments, they will judge us as doing what we should, as opposed to those of the world, who will judge us unrighteously.

*Therefore let us not sleep, as do others; but **let us watch** and be sober.*

(Side note: sobriety in the scriptures does not always refer to abstention from alcohol, but also to commandment keeping! It is a Hebrew idiom, just as drunkenness refers to lawlessness all throughout the writings of the prophets.)

And so for our family, Sukkot is a birthday party for Yeshua. We have cake and ice cream and party favors on that High Sabbath and we thank the Father for sending Him. We give to the poor instead of to each other (one of the hallmarks of biblical feasts is that we are to give gifts to the poor, which makes way more sense than giving stuff to people who are well off and don't even need (or generally want) what we give them).

Sukkot also has a future prophetic fulfillment, it is a 7 day Feast, and is a picture of Yeshua coming once again to the earth to rule and reign for 1000 years during the 7th Millennium. And nothing, brothers and sisters, should be more exciting than that.

The prophet Zechariah said that we will keep this Feast even during the Millennial reign of Yeshua!

*Zech 14:16 And it shall come to pass, that every one that is left of all the nations which came against Jerusalem shall even go up from year to year to worship the King, the LORD of hosts, and to keep the feast of tabernacles.*

So when we keep this Feast, we are making a proclamation that the Messiah has come, born of a virgin, on the Feast of Tabernacles, a day of prophetic meaning, and we also declare our absolute belief that on that Feast in the future, He will begin to rule and reign for 1000 years on the earth just as He promised![113] Halleluyah!

---

[113] Rev 20:4

## The Fall Feasts Pt 4 – HaShanna Rabbah

HaShanna Rabbah, a High Sabbath occurring the day after the Feast of Sukkot, is also called "The Last Great Day." This would have been the 8th day after Yeshua's birth and He would have been taken by His father Joseph to be circumcised.[114] This is the day He formally entered into all the Covenants of promise.[115]

This is the day of the year when, more than any other, Jews would have been outside the Temple reciting prayers that Messiah would come soon! Come Messiah! As Yeshua was formally entering into the Covenant, they were crying out for Him and their prayers were being answered!

This is also the day when Jews believe that judgments are executed against people, the judgments which were determined on Yom Kippur against the unrepentant. So it is appropriate that on this day (which can also simply be seen as the last day of Sukkot), we believe that the Great Throne Judgment will take place against all mankind, both great and small, after the 1000 year reign of Yeshua. Again, a future prophetic fulfillment will occur.

See that?

1.  Sukkot – 1000 year reign, followed directly by
2.  Hashanna Rabbah – the Judgment throne

Just like in the book of Revelation.

When we keep HaShanna Rabbah, it is a declaration that things will happen exactly according to the prophecies of scripture concerning the judgment. It is our statement of faith that someday, true justice will be done in all matters.

---

[114] Lev 12:3
[115] Eph 2:12

*see www.theancientbridge.com for the rewrite of this chapter*

## What About Christmas and Easter?

Remember I told you about Deuteronomy 12:32, forbidding us to add and subtract from God's laws like the Pharisees did? Well, we've done it too, or at least we've inherited what others did and lived by it, much like the Orthodox Jews of today inherited the laws of the Pharisees. And I look at what they do, not with contempt but with the realization that they inherited things just the same as we did, and they haven't ditched their traditions any more than Christians have.

In fact, right now I want to make something very clear. I do not have anything but positive feelings about Jews and Christians, and I have to give credit where credit is due. Observant Jews care more deeply about obeying God than anyone on earth, there is a zealousness that I deeply admire and it touches my heart. Their dedication to family is simply amazing, and their dedication to the scriptures is incredible.

Do you want to know why the Jews survived the Black Death that devastated Christians throughout the world? Christians were not washing their hands in those days or bathing, but the Jews were. I mean that seriously. It became so evident that Jews were not dying of plague that people began accusing the Jews of witchcraft! But it was their laws far in excess of what was written that we follow as good hygiene practices today (I have to add however, that this was not done for hygiene purposes but for holiness). So it is a good idea to wash hands, but as far as them calling ritual hand washing an actual commandment of God, that is incorrect. For the record, they were not simply washing their hands, but they also recited a prayer as they did it, and had to do it according to a specific ritual which is also practiced today. Here is the prayer.

"Blessed art Thou, O Lord our God, King of the universe, who has sanctified us with Thy commandments and has commanded us concerning the washing of the hands."

Now there is no commandment to do this in scripture, so this can only be justified as a commandment of the Talmud.

205

How about Christianity?  There are more people being cared for around the world because of everyday Christians than I could write about in a thousand books – orphanages built and maintained, sex slaves rescued from the streets, hospitals built, abused women and children sheltered, the list just goes on and on, things that we cannot just ignore, done in the name of Jesus.

But each faith has a legacy of adding to the commandments of God their own traditions and judging people based on them.  Each faith has added and subtracted as they see fit.

Christmas and Easter are on the top of that list for Christians.  The verses preceding Deut 12:32 are very sobering verses indeed.  And I ask you to consider them carefully, because Christmas is a tradition, not a commandment of God, and Easter is a tradition, not a commandment of God – just like ritual hand washing.  We should never judge, nor hate another person based on their nonconformance to our traditions because if we do, we will do violence to one another (even if it is only in our hearts) as *some* of the Pharisee leaders plotted to do violence to Yeshua because He challenged the traditions that they enforced as authoritative laws.

*Deut 12:28-32* **Observe and hear all these words which I command thee,** *that it may go well with thee, and with thy children after thee* **forever***, when thou doest that which is good and right in the sight of the* Lord *thy God.*

*When the* Lord *thy God shall cut off the nations from before thee, whither thou goest to possess them, and thou succeedest them, and dwellest in their land;*

*Take heed to thyself that thou* **be not snared by following them***, after that they be destroyed from before thee; and that thou* **enquire not after their gods***, saying,* **How did these nations serve their gods? even so will I do likewise.**

*Thou shalt not do so unto the LORD thy God: for every abomination to the LORD, which he hateth, have they done unto their gods; for even their sons and their daughters they have burnt in the fire to their gods.*

*What thing soever I command you, observe to do it:* **thou shalt not add thereto, nor diminish from it.**

First verse, He reiterates that His commandments are forever. Then He warned them not to find out about anything related to the paganism of the nations they were going to destroy, and do it in order to worship Him. He called every single thing they do for their gods an abomination. It's His absolute harshest word for the things He hates. Then He says, in a nutshell, that His laws are good as they are and have no need to be added to or subtracted from.

Passover is enough
Unleavened Bread is enough
First Fruits is enough
Shavuot is enough
Yom Teruah is enough
Sukkot is enough
HaShannah Rabbah is enough.

Easter replaced the Spring Feasts and so we lost sight of God's prophetic plan and calendar, leaving us blind and unable to explain or even truly understand what Yeshua did and fulfilled. It left us unable to explain to our Jewish brothers and sisters why Yeshua is not an idolater and a blasphemer.

Christmas replaced the Fall Feasts, and so we became blind there as well to what He will do and will fulfill. The end will largely come upon the church like a thief, because we have not been aware of the times and seasons.

And I understand not wanting to abandon them because of the memories associated with them and because of the fear of family disapproval. And yes, it will happen, people won't understand – and they will judge you for not keeping their traditions. But that is what they are – traditions. When we judge people by traditions, and value the traditions more than we value the truth, we become like the people who conspired to kill Yeshua.

Traditions blind. Whereas people do not get angry if you break a commandment, they will get angry if you question their tradition, because to break a tradition is to challenge someone's life choices, while to break a commandment is to challenge God. People will take it personally, and this is why we have to choose who we will serve. I speak from heartache and experience on this.

No one is telling you to ditch your memories, just to put them into proper perspective. It was always difficult for everyone coming into Covenant to leave their cultures behind in order to follow YHVH, in fact it was so difficult that when Moses delayed in coming back down from the mountain, the people demanded that Aaron, Moses' own brother, make them a golden calf that they could worship (the Egyptians worshipped Hathor and Apis, cattle gods). And this is what Aaron did –

*Ex 32:4-5 And he received them at their hand, and fashioned it with a graving tool, after he had made it a molten calf: and they said,* **These be thy gods, O Israel, which brought thee up out of the land of Egypt.**

*[5] And when Aaron saw it, he built an altar before it; and Aaron made proclamation, and said,* **Tomorrow is a feast to the LORD.**

It wasn't just that Aaron made something attached to that abominable Egyptian paganism, but He set up a feast on a day never commanded and said it was to, in the Hebrew, YHVH. YHVH was so angry that He threatened to kill them all, saying that they had corrupted themselves. This was a very serious betrayal, considering what YHVH had done for them.

But isn't that what Christmas is? When we detach ourselves from the emotional aspects of the holiday, from our fond memories, didn't our forefathers simply take a golden calf and announce a feast to YHVH?

I can't force you to give up those holidays. I can't even force you to want to give them up. But I ask you very bluntly, what does YHVH deserve from us in terms of loyalty? Is it to keep His Feasts His way, or to do things our way and expect Him to approve? Do we truly honor Him when we do what we want when we want? The scriptures, from front to back, say no.

## Circumcision of the Heart vs Circumcision of the Flesh

One of the unfortunate things we have been taught is that certain Bible things are an "either/or" scenario instead of an "and" scenario. Would it shock you that the first place we see a commandment to circumcise the heart is in the Torah? It sure shocked me!

First I am going to show you a commonly quoted verse – but then we have to do my favorite thing – keep on reading!

*Deut 10:12-16 **And now, Israel, what doth the LORD thy God require of thee,** but to fear the LORD thy God, to walk in all his ways, and to love him, and to serve the LORD thy God with all thy heart and with all thy soul,*

***To keep the commandments of the LORD, and his statutes, which I command thee this day for thy good?***

*Behold, the heaven and the heaven of heavens is the LORD's thy God, the earth also, with all that therein is.*

*Only the LORD had a delight in thy fathers to love them, and he chose their seed after them, even you above all people, as it is this day.*

***Circumcise therefore the foreskin of your heart, and be no more stiffnecked.***

I don't know about you, but I was never taught the rest of the story. It wasn't, "Circumcise your flesh if you are a Jew and your heart if you are a Christian," it has always been, "Circumcise your flesh AND your heart if you love Him"

It is mentioned two more times –

*Deut 30:6* **And the L**ORD **thy God will circumcise thine heart,** *and the heart of thy seed, to love the* LORD *thy God with all thine heart, and with all thy soul, that thou mayest live.*

The context of this is a prophetic announcement of Israel's future repentance after falling away into idolatry, which did happen. When Yeshua came in order that the gospel of the Kingdom would be preached to the world, which included these lost sons of Israel, many received the indwelling of the Holy Spirit, which, when mixed with our obedience, is doing the very painful work of circumcising our hearts. One more –

*Jer 4:4* **Circumcise yourselves to the L**ORD**, and take away the foreskins of your heart,** *ye men of Judah and inhabitants of Jerusalem: lest my fury come forth like fire, and burn that none can quench it, because of the evil of your doings.*

Here, before the destruction of Jerusalem, YHVH pleads through the prophet Jeremiah for the people of Israel to circumcise their own hearts – but how?

*Jer 4:1-2 If thou wilt return, O Israel, saith the* LORD*, return unto me: and if thou wilt* **put away thine abominations** *out of my sight, then shalt thou not remove. And* **thou shalt swear, The L**ORD **liveth, in truth, in judgment, and in righteousness;** *and the nations shall bless themselves in him, and in him shall they glory.*

We have already established that His character does not allow Him to give impossible or unreasonable commands, therefore this was definitely doable, but they were so stiff-necked and hated God's laws so much (and by extension, they hated Him), that they would not do righteousness.

So, if we are not willing to give up certain things God says are bad or make Him unhappy, are our hearts truly circumcised? Imagine a man who refuses to even pull his pants down, could he possibly be circumcised in the flesh? Same with the circumcision of the heart, if we are stiff-necked, it is not going to happen.

The circumcision of the heart is an integral part of the teachings of Judaism. The process of being fundamentally changed through humility, submission and love is very central to the tenants of Judaism – and is most certainly not a Christian concept, but one of divine origins from the very beginning.

## But the Commandments are Written on My Heart

We were taught this, but this is another case where we have to read for context, because a very important promise hinges on all of this

*Jer 31:31-37 Behold, the days come, saith the* LORD, *that I will make a **new covenant with the house of Israel, and with the house of Judah:*** (side bar – notice there is no Covenant with the Gentiles, who must be grafted in and become a part of the combined Commonwealth of Israel)

*Not according to the covenant that I made with their fathers in the day that I took them by the hand to bring them out of the land of Egypt; which my covenant they brake, although I was an husband unto them, saith the* LORD:

*But this shall be the covenant that I will make with the house of Israel; **After those days**, saith the* LORD, ***I will put my law in their inward parts, and write it in their hearts**; and will be their God, and they shall be my people.*

*And **they shall teach no more every man his neighbour, and every man his brother, saying, Know the* LORD: *for they shall all know me,** from the least of them unto the greatest of them, saith the* LORD: *for I will forgive their iniquity, and I will remember their sin no more.*

***If those ordinances depart from before me**, saith the* LORD, *then **the seed of Israel also shall cease from being a nation before me for ever.***

*Thus saith the* LORD; ***If heaven above can be measured**, and the foundations of the earth searched out beneath, **I will also cast off all the seed of Israel** for all that they have done, saith the* LORD.

This is entirely a future prophecy.  How do we know?  Because we still need teachers.  Not all people know Him.

At the time of the manifestation of this prophecy (which I believe will commence during the Millennial reign "after those days"), all will know Him because He will be the King of the world! It will be kind of hard to deny it at that point.

There is a question that begs to be answered, "Why would God put His law in our inward parts, and write it on our hearts, if we are not supposed to obey it, if indeed it was not good?" What would be the point? If something is on my heart, I do it. If you are sad, and it is on my heart to call you, I either do it or prove that it wasn't really on my heart at all. It is the same with giving money to a beggar or rescuing a lost kitten. Our actions, and not our words, prove what is in our hearts. That is the essence of Hebrew thought. Greeks think about things, Hebrews hear and then do. In Greek thought, one would meditate on how much they love someone but in Hebrew thought, they would do something to prove it. Or to put it another way, philosophers ponder, and Jews do something about what they are pondering. We should have the same attitude as the Jews!

From this passage, we also see that the Torah laws will be the governing laws of His future Kingdom. Why? Because He says that if His laws ever depart, then Israel as a people will cease to exist. We know that this has not happened. If Israel has been cast aside, then how do we explain away Paul's statement?

*Romans 11:26a And so all Israel shall be saved*

## YHVH Made Our Bodies to be Healthy

Many of God's laws positively impact our health, via the setting-apart of our bodies through what we put in them and how we care for them in general. Don't drink blood (of course, this also had ties to pagan worship), don't eat the thick animal fat from cows, sheep and goats, bathe when you come in contact with blood or sickness or have sex. Pretty much, we already do this because it's just common sense. We recognize these are sensible laws. But Leviticus 11 covers laws that our modern minds don't recognize as sensible, like the ban on eating "garbage disposal" animals.

All the fish, birds, and land animals YHVH created are good, He said so Himself on day 5 and 6 of creation. But different animals are good for different things, and there is a whole class of animals that exist as garbage disposals (which is good!) and as such, their meat is naturally toxic – no matter how thoroughly you cook them. Let me tell you about my first day of Torah pursuit.

I was sitting in front of my computer on June 4, 2011 when I heard YHVH speak to me through His Spirit.

"So, you want to explain to me all these verses that say you can eat pork?"

I was stunned, and my heart sank and I got sick to my stomach – I could smell the morning bacon and never once in all my years as a believer has He ever issued a challenge to anything I ended up being right about. But I sure gave it the old college try, and like always, I tested the Spirit against the Word.

What did I find out? First I found out what some modern translations added. Namely, the parenthetical statement found in Mark 7:19 claiming that Jesus declared all foods clean.

You can't find it until the 20th century in a single Bible. Some modern translators added to the word of God by taking a parenthetical statement from an obscure manuscript and made a verse about ritual Pharisaic hand washing appear like it is a ruling on food – a blasphemous one at that, inferring that Yeshua sinned by changing the law. I wish I could say that was the only time that modern translators added to or subtracted from the Bible, but it isn't. I am not a KJV only, but whenever they add something, they usually admit it by putting it in italics. So at least we know.

As I shared before, Acts 10 doesn't cleanse anything that is unclean. And there are other verses as well, but it boils down to this – the Bible must be allowed to interpret the Bible and Leviticus 11 defines what food is and isn't, period. Every author of the New Testament, except Luke, was born in a Jewish home, and when they said food, their definition was according to Lev 11 and not according to any other culture. When an American says the word food, it would not mean horse or dog; this is the same exact concept.

Back to my story, the whole family gave up pork, rabbit, and shellfish and any fish without fins and scales. I was 41 and had three medical conditions – high blood pressure, asthma, and arthritis. In fact, my fingers were already curling and had been for a decade. I had let my prescription lapse and when I went to the doctor three weeks later, we found that my blood pressure was normal, and once I thought about it, there I was in the California Central Valley and I had not used my inhaler in three weeks, and my fingers didn't hurt. Within a few months, with the exception of the ring finger on my right hand, they were straight as nails. To this day, I have never had a problem with asthma again. And all I did was eat only clean meats. All I did was trust God and tell my flesh to take a hike.

## Can I Please Have a Cheeseburger?

One of the biggest misconceptions about Torah law is that you cannot mix meat and dairy (any form of dairy, including butter, cheese, yogurt, sour cream, etc.) because of one verse, repeated three times. And I am going to tell you up front that a lot of people disagree with me on this. Again, you make up your own mind and do your own research – I will simply tell you what the Bible says because that is all I can do.

*Thou shalt not seethe a kid in its mothers milk.*[116]

And you may be saying, "I don't see cheese or meat mentioned anywhere, except that a kid (baby goat) is made of meat." Well, this is how rabbinical law works sometimes. Even though archaeologists have tied the boiling of a baby goat in the milk of its mother to be a Caananite fertility ritual,[117] keeping milk and meat separate is established halakah. It's the same with Christian tradition; we often refuse to give them up even when confronted with incontrovertible proof of original intent. And like anything else, anyone who keeps this rabbinical ruling has their reasons – and it is not sin for them to not eat milk and meat together. But I would fervently disagree that anyone has the right to enforce this as Torah law.

But if the archaeological evidence and what is clearly written is not enough, we can see that Abraham served the three strangers, one of which was YHVH, milk and meat together, and they ate it.

*Gen 18:7-8 And Abraham ran unto the herd, and fetcht a calf tender and good, and gave it unto a young man; and he hasted to dress it.*

---

[116] Ex 23:19, 34:26, Deut 14:21

[117] Jackson, Wayne, *The Ras Shamra Discovery (Montgomery, AL: Apologetics Press)*
http://www.apologeticspress.org/rr/reprints/Ras-Shamra.pdf

*And he took **butter, and milk, and the calf** which he had dressed, and* **set it before them**; *and he stood by them under the tree,* **and they did eat.**

YHVH does not sin.  He ate milk and meat together.  We can too.

So as far as I am concerned, I'll have a cheeseburger.  Make it a double!

## Kosher Diet vs Biblical Diet

They aren't the same – eating Biblically is much easier, not to mention cheaper.

No, everything you eat does not have to display the kosher symbol; it just has to contain clean ingredients as defined by the Torah.[118] It takes time to learn it all and every once in a while we all blow it and eat something with pork based gelatin (like marshmallows or jello), or lard (like store bought pie crusts), or chicken sausage that was encased in pig intestine, but the point is that we keep on going and not get defeated.

Eating biblically includes plants, and most of the animals at the supermarket. All types of birds sold at supermarkets in the US are Biblically allowed – it isn't until you get into carrion birds that you have a problem. So that means chickens, turkeys, game hens, ducks and geese are fine. Most types of animals sold at US supermarkets are also fine. Beef, Lamb, Goat, Deer, Elk, Buffalo, and Moose are all clean animals. Any fish with fins and scales is great, but it takes a while to learn which is which. Animals to be shunned at the supermarket are pigs, rabbits, shellfish, catfish, squid (calamari), and shark.

Leviticus chap 11 defines, as far as meat goes, what is clean and unclean – what is food and what is not food. "Garbage disposal" animals (bottom feeders) are unclean, and their meat is toxic. I have a shellfish allergy, because my body is not able to digest the toxin they produce. Honestly, I don't want to tax my body by making it digest toxins anyway! The toxicity of the unclean animals is easily verified through research. And we may not understand why certain animals are forbidden for food. Sometimes YHVH asks us to do things that only He understands and

---

[118] www.theisraelofgodrc.com/CUPL.html is a wonderful website dedicated to helping believers know which store bought foods contain clean and unclean ingredients.

carrying out His orders is faith, or as I call it "belief in action," because faith without works (doing something to prove it) is dead.[119]

In order to be "kosher" the butcher has to follow rabbinical halakah, and slaughter the animal a certain way, draining out all the blood. The commandment not to eat blood is given many times in scripture and is included in the Acts 15 basic guidelines for incoming believers.

Now, in some countries, the blood is not drained, but here in the US it is. Blood is a very valuable ingredient in the manufacturing of pet food, a cheap source of nutrients, so they make sure they drain the animals. Because of that, I am very comfortable buying my meat at the grocery store until I find a valid reason not to. Everyone has to make their own call. I do not ask or tell you to do things my way.

Some people, based on a misconception, salt their meat in order to "draw out the blood." But biologically this makes no sense at all, because blood is confined within the veins and the only things that pass from the bloodstream into the muscle are oxygen and nutrients (things at a molecular level). In addition, people will often claim that meat must be cooked well done to "drive out the blood." However, meat "juice" is not blood, it is a protein called myoglobin, which is pigmented read and gives the meat its reddish shade. I highly encourage you to check this out for yourself before someone confuses you. And even if that red juice was blood, cooking the meat to well-done would not drive out the blood, it would simply cook it. And we are not allowed to eat cooked blood any more than we are permitted to eat raw blood!

In addition to blood, we are also not to eat the excess fat of the "slaughtering animals" – cows, sheep and goats. So just keep it lean and you will be fine – and leaner too!

---

[119] James 2:20

Eating biblically just takes practice. Unless you are already a vegetarian, you are going to make mistakes. As in everything, I pray you will extend yourself the same amount of patient grace that I am trying so hard to communicate to you. It's so incredibly important to see this through a Father's eyes.

## Niddah – Sending Your Wife Out of Town for a Week – NOT!

First of all, I am not going to tell you how to observe this or any other law -- that's your business.  My entire purpose is to address what is and is not written, because frankly there are a lot of misconceptions out there.  A whole lot of folks get upset because of what they think is written in Leviticus 15.  And right now we are only taking about a normal menstruation cycle here, and not the issue of abnormal bleeding, which is entirely different, and points to a serious medical condition.

*19 And if a woman have an issue, and her issue in her flesh be blood, she shall be put apart seven days: and whosoever toucheth her shall be unclean until the even.*
*20 And every thing that she lieth upon in her separation shall be unclean: every thing also that she sitteth upon shall be unclean.*
*21 And whosoever toucheth her bed shall wash his clothes, and bathe himself in water, and be unclean until the even.*
*22 And whosoever toucheth any thing that she sat upon shall wash his clothes, and bathe himself in water, and be unclean until the even.*
*23 And if it be on her bed, or on any thing whereon she sitteth, when he toucheth it, he shall be unclean until the even.*
*24 And if any man lie with her at all, and her flowers be upon him, he shall be unclean seven days; and all the bed whereon he lieth shall be unclean.*

First misconception -- uncleanness is a sin.  Where does it say this?  Nowhere.  Uncleanness is a **condition** that must be remedied before one goes to the Tabernacle/Temple.  I will give the verse telling why a bit later.  YHVH did not create us to be sinful without any hope.  If uncleanness were a sin, then any woman with a sexually overactive husband would be ritually unclean every day of her life, and therefore in sin!  No, uncleanness was simply something that had to be dealt with, and the remedy was simple -- bathe and wait until evening and then one was able to go to the Temple.  No biggie.  Seriously, this wasn't a big deal.

Second misconception – touching someone unclean, or being touched by them, is a sin.  Oh I know people like to use this verse entirely out of context, from II Corinthians 6:17 *Wherefore come out from among them, and be ye separate, saith the Lord, and touch not the unclean thing; and I will receive you."*  But the entire context of that was idolatry, not natural body functions! Yeshua touched unclean lepers[120] so there could be no question of sinfulness.  Nowhere are we forbidden to touch the unclean.

Third misconception -- women have to live separately during their periods.  Some folks really get upset about this one, but what does "put apart" mean?  "Put apart" in the KJV is literally the word "niddah" and it means separation or set apartness related to uncleanness.  In other words, the menstrual woman had a special status -- she was not the same as she was the rest of the month.  Sexually she was untouchable (Lev 18:19), and so in essence she was separated.  Was there a commandment for her to live elsewhere?  No.  Was there a commandment not to touch her?  No.  What there was, was a specific commandment of what to do if you did touch her or the things she laid or sat on during her period.  It is a set apart time, a different time, a time to be aware.

Fourth misconception -- the couch she sits on and her bed need to be cleaned.  I've had this one thrown in my face, "Oh yeah, do you wash the couches?"  They say this (generally with a smirk) because some versions of the Bible have a different rendering of Mark 7:4 than we see in the KJV *"And when they come from the market, except they wash,*

---

[120] Matt 8:3

*they eat not. And many other things there be, which they have received to hold, as the washing of cups, and pots, brasen vessels, and of tables."* Instead of table, the word couch is used, which it indeed can mean. But as we see here, Yeshua is clearly referring the Oral Torah commandments surrounding the preparation and eating of food and not actual Torah commandments. As you see from above, no, there is no commandment to steam clean the bed and couches.

Fifth misconception -- men and women are only at risk of being unclean during niddah.

*16 And if any man's seed of copulation go out from him, then he shall wash all his flesh in water, and be unclean until the even.*
*17 And every garment, and every skin, whereon is the seed of copulation, shall be washed with water, and be unclean until the even.*
*18 The woman also with whom man shall lie with seed of copulation, they shall both bathe themselves in water, and be unclean until the even.*

That's right, normal everyday sex makes you unclean as well, with the exact same remedy! God would not command us to be fruitful and multiply if it were His desire for us to be ritually clean 24/7. Ritual uncleanness is never a problem EXCEPT for special circumstances -- like going up to the Temple for the feasts or sacrifices or to serve, or when one is about to do battle in the Name of YHVH, as we see in Joshua.

Niddah is about awareness, not about shunning. Niddah teaches us when to and not to come into the Temple, and what steps have to be taken in order to be clean again. Sin would be going up to the Temple in an unclean state, and because everyone knew what it took to make one unclean, this was easily avoided. Here is the specific verse that sums it all up.

*31 Thus shall ye separate the children of Israel from their uncleanness;* **that they die not in their uncleanness, when they defile my tabernacle that is among them.**

There you have it -- don't go to the Temple unclean!  As for the bathing, who doesn't want to bathe (I mean, besides our children)? Uncleanness boils down to one simple thing, a **temporary** disqualification from going to the Temple.

And we must remember that during ancient times (as well as today), not having blood properly taken care of was dangerous to everyone. See -- another health benefit!  Frankly, in ancient times one's menstruation would have been quite an ordeal, I am so glad we are alive now when it is much easier!

Almost all of the misconceptions about this law are related to what people hear about how the Orthodox Jews do things, separation for 14 days, separate beds, etc. but once again, read what the Bible does and does not say, and the truth shall set you free.  Keeping this law according to the Talmud can be extremely demoralizing for women who were not raised this way, making a difficult time of the month far worse than it has to be, especially when one does not already possess the mindsets and cultural attitudes of the Jews.

## Sexual Immorality

Leviticus 18 is our go-to chapter on forbidden sexual acts. Rape is covered elsewhere and I am not going to insult you by unneeded focus on incest or bestiality or child sacrifice – you are Christians, you have no illusions about any of those things being even remotely acceptable. In fact, I will only bring up two laws here: one because it is creeping into the church by leaps and bounds and the other because it isn't being kept, much to the detriment of a woman's dignity, and possibly, health.

*Lev 18:22 And do not lie with a male as with a female, it is an abomination.*

It has become fashionable to ignore this one – and as far as people outside of the Body of Messiah, I believe we should ignore it. They are not members of the Covenant, and have not agreed to live according to its tenets. We have no right to enforce this law on them above all others. In fact, nowhere in scripture does it tell us to focus our attentions on the lawlessness of the unsaved, but only on the Body! The world is always going to behave like the world, and it is fruitless to be so constantly offended and shocked by that. That doesn't mean that we should cooperate with them in their sin, or aid them in it, but it does mean that we need to respect their personal boundaries while also enforcing our personal boundaries. I won't buy someone a ham sandwich and I will not allow them to guilt me into doing it, but I won't go into their home and empty their fridge of pork either; I don't have the right to do that.

And it doesn't matter if they were "born this way" or became that way through genetics or choice or any other condition. We do not allow pedophiles to prey on children, or sociopaths to murder people, just because they say they have always been that way. Truthfully, we were all born with a natural predilection for sin, a delight in it – whether the "big" ones or the "small" ones.

I don't hate homosexuals; I hate any sin *in the Body* accepted as good, whether it is eating pork and shellfish, or sabbath breaking, or idolatry or homosexuality. I don't hate one more than the other – what I hate is people taking it upon themselves to call good evil, evil good, clean unclean and unclean clean once they know better, in order to be more socially acceptable.

The second law I want to briefly discuss, because a lot of us didn't even know was there.

*Lev 18:19 And do not approach a woman to uncover her nakedness in her monthly separation of uncleanness.*

We have already discussed the importance of keeping one's blood to oneself. Did you now that cervical cancer rates among Jewish women are incredibly low? For a long time they chalked it up to circumcision, but have ruled it out and some doctors are turning their attention to the abstention from sex during one's period.

In addition, a woman's time of the month can be a very uncomfortable time, and I believe that it was YHVH's intention that her dignity be maintained, as well as her health. Going 7 days without sex isn't going to kill anyone, and might just save a life. A woman's body deserves its rest.

## Tzitzit – The Most Outward Sign of Who We Belong to

No doubt about it, if you wear tzitzit, people will ask you if you are Jewish! But it's really the greatest witnessing opportunity ever. Imagine someone coming up to you in the store to preach the gospel to you because they think you are Jewish, and you get to share the entire Bible. I've done it. The commandment to wear them is in Numbers 15

*37-40 The LORD said to Moses, "Speak to the Israelites and say to them: 'Throughout the generations to come you are to make tassels on the corners of your garments, with a **blue cord** on each tassel. **You will have these tassels to look at and so you will remember all the commands of the LORD**, that you may obey them and not prostitute yourselves by chasing after the lusts of your own hearts and eyes. **Then you will remember to obey all my commands and will be consecrated to your God.***

The tzitzit, more than anything else, set us apart in the eyes of the world as belonging exclusively to YHVH. They not only help us to remember the commandments, but from personal experience, I behave myself more when wearing them because I know that everyone sees what I do as a reflection of my King. I do not want to dishonor Him through my bad behavior. I want to bring Him glory. And yes I do wear them – it says Israelites, not men, it isn't exclusive (again, this is a matter of much debate). The only requirement for them is that they be tassels with a blue cord included. Rabbinical laws say they have to be done with a certain dye and tied in a certain way, but the Word does not say this. Stick with the word until YHVH tells you otherwise. Keep it simple, this walk is supposed to be freedom from bondage.

## To Tithe or Not to Tithe

This is actually a funny question – because tithing is "Old Testament Law" and cannot be justified outside of it. Yet the tithe is preached as an ultimatum even when the rest of the law is denigrated. In the New Testament, we see freewill offerings towards the apostles and the poor, which has always been practiced. The tithe is also mentioned by Yeshua as being good,[121] so let's look at it in context.

The tithe served a specific function in ancient Israel. The Levites were not allotted an inheritance like the rest of the Tribes, with private land and the opportunities that afforded. They had their own cities and pastures, but their primary purpose in life was serving YHVH and the Nation. During the 40 years in the wilderness, specific groups were responsible for carrying certain parts of the Tabernacle as the Nation travelled from place to place, and the sons of Aaron served in the Tabernacle or Temple itself.

As such, it was the responsibility of the Nation to support them with their tithes, in the form of the first fruits of their harvest. In this way, they never suffered lack – as long as the people obeyed the commandment.

*Numbers 18:21-24: "And **to the sons of Levi**, behold, **I have given all the tithe in Israel for an inheritance**, in return for their service which they perform, the service of the tent of meeting. And the sons of Israel shall not come near the tent of meeting again, lest they bear sin and die. Only the Levites shall perform the service of the tent of meeting, and they shall bear their iniquity; **it shall be a perpetual statute throughout your generations,** and among the sons of Israel they shall have no inheritance. For the tithe of the sons of Israel, which they offer as an offering to the Lord, I have given to the Levites for an inheritance; therefore I have said concerning them, 'They shall have no inheritance among the sons of Israel.'"*

---

[121] Matt 23:23

We have no right to say that what was specifically designated for one group now belongs to another when YHVH said that it was a perpetual statute for the Levites, but that is what modern pastors have done. Even some pastors who have moved to pursuing Torah now say that they are doing the work of the Levites. But they are often not doing the work of the Levites, whose duties are clearly spelled out and generally they are not even genetically Levites. This is what is called "Replacement Theology" -- taking what belongs to one group and transferring it to another without a "Thus saith the LORD." The tithe served the purpose of taking care of the tribe that had no inheritance in the land, no ability to gather land and accumulate wealth; it was used to feed the poor, widows and orphans, and to provide money for the individual celebration of the feasts.

I am not against giving, but when someone tells you to tithe to them, ask them if they are a Levite, or if they are even biblically eligible to perform the Levitical functions spelled out in scripture. Support those teaching you, by all means, and support the poor, the widows and the orphans (who were also to be the recipients of the tithe[122]). But do not think that supporting pastors on salary and building larger buildings is the same thing as fulfilling the Levitical tithe commandment. The tithe is specifically designated by YHVH, for YHVH's purposes, and we don't have the right to change what He said.

As soon as the altar is rebuilt and the Levites are serving at it again and serving as teachers of the Torah, I will honor them with tithes for doing the work YHVH has called them to, but biblically, not just anyone has the right to it. Like many Torah issues, this is subject to debate within the Body and there is nothing wrong with a healthy and respectful debate.

The bottom line is this. Regardless of whether or not the tithe is in practical effect in modern times, the truth is that when we bless and honor the people who teach and minister to us, we are blessing and honoring our King who sent them out. When we take financial care of

---

[122] Deut 26:12

234

the poor, the widows and the orphans, we are showing the heart of our Father.  Call it the spirit of the tithe law, if you will, but we have an obligation to always honor the King in everything we do.

## But I Don't Want to Marry My Brother in Law!

Levirate Marriage was a law intended to preserve inheritance rights and ensure the position of a dead man's wife within his family. In the Land, each tribe had its own allotments, which would pass down from father to sons, with the first born getting a double portion. An understanding of Levirate marriage is essential to understanding what happened with Ruth and Boaz, as well as the situation with Judah's sons in Genesis 38. Tamar married Judah's oldest son Er, knowing full well that her sons would benefit from the double portion inheritance. When Er died and his younger brother refused to impregnate her, it was for one reason and one reason only – if Tamar died childless, he would inherit the double portion, instead of her child (who would by rights receive it). Tamar needed that standing within the family or she might forever be a widow in her father's house, childless and without position. The Levirate marriage was not only for the sake of the dead man's name being carried on, but also for the sake of providing for his widow!

The Levirate marriage ensured a woman's place in the family for all time. In a way, she became the inheritor in place of her husband until her children reached adulthood.

*Deut 25:5 If brethren dwell together, and one of them die, and have no child, the wife of the dead shall not marry without unto a **stranger**: her husband's brother shall go in unto her, and take her to him to wife, and perform the duty of an husband's brother unto her.*

I see no commandment that the woman has to marry her brother in law, but a commandment that he has an obligation to take her as a wife. Biblically, strangers fall into the category of "zur" or "ger." Deut 24:5 speaks of "zur," strangers to the Covenant, as opposed to "ger" who are not native born, and yet keep the Covenant in all things except circumcision. As marrying someone who is not an Israelite is forbidden anyway, this is not a new law imposed upon the widow. As the inheritance system which made this law necessary is no longer in place, Levirate marriage is not practiced in modern times.

## I've Heard That the Torah Forbids Interracial Relations

Well, yes and no. If you are referring to races as in different species, yes that is definitely forbidden. However, every union between a male and a female of the human race is allowed as long as they are not close relations. The only prohibition is to not take for a husband or wife someone who is not a believer.

*Deut 7:1-4 When the* LORD *thy God shall bring thee into the land whither thou goest to possess it, and hath cast out many nations before thee, the Hittites, and the Girgashites, and the Amorites, and the Canaanites, and the Perizzites, and the Hivites, and the Jebusites, seven nations greater and mightier than thou;*

*And when the* LORD *thy God shall deliver them before thee; thou shalt smite them, and utterly destroy them; thou shalt make no covenant with them, nor shew mercy unto them:*

***Neither shalt thou make marriages with them; thy daughter thou shalt not give unto his son, nor his daughter shalt thou take unto thy son.***

***For they will turn away thy son from following me, that they may serve other gods: so will the anger of the*** LORD ***be kindled against you, and destroy thee suddenly.***

Israelites, then and now, are all colors, and always will be. Along with the children of Israel was a mixed multitude of people who had left Egypt – I imagine there were people from every single nation Egypt had enslaved, including many Egyptians. I know more "interracial" couples since pursuing Torah than I ever did in the rest of my life put together. We are united by the Word and Yeshua, and the color stops mattering.

As an aside, it has been my experience that mixed religion marriages are generally peaceful enough until children come along, or until someone actually wants to practice their religion, and then two people who didn't care about religion begin to care very deeply and usually there is either a mixture (which is forbidden) or a complete capitulation by one party (often the follower of Messiah hoping to influence their spouse by compromising everything). Anything that diverts us from the narrow path is deadly, if we believe what we say we believe – which is that Yeshua is the way, the truth and the life, and that there is no way to the Father besides Him.

Generally, when we knowingly marry someone with a different faith, we are giving them permission not to take ours seriously. And if we are serious about God, it becomes a very lonely life, no matter how warm and fuzzy our feelings were at the beginning.

We do not have a right to force our beliefs on the person we married – after all, if we come into an understanding of the Torah long after our marriage and they refuse to live that way, they are really only guilty of being exactly the same person we fell in love with and married. We don't have the right to expect differently. They are still who they said they were, while we are the ones who changed. So be patient, and perhaps your good character and obedience will inspire them.

## You Can't Seriously Tell Me That God Wants Me to Marry a Rapist!

Super unfortunate translation! Just awful. No, this is a law protecting a woman from being seduced and abandoned. If a man seduced a woman, and they then went on to have consensual sex, he was required to pay the bride price and marry her *forever*. He could never divorce her. As she was willingly seduced, this should not be a disagreeable arrangement for her and it discouraged men from seducing women they were not willing to stay with forever.

*Deut 22:28-29 If a man find a damsel that is a virgin, which is not betrothed, and lay hold on her, and lie with her, and they be found;*

*Then the man that lay with her shall give unto the damsel's father fifty shekels of silver, and she shall be his wife; because he hath humbled her, he may not put her away all his days.*

That word translated "lay hold" is taphas – whose chief meaning is "manipulate" or in other words, seduce. If this were not the case, then there would be no need whatsoever for a Ketubah (marriage contract) because a disgusting, vile person could simply spy out a gorgeous, unbetrothed virgin, rape her and get to keep her. From what we see throughout the Torah, this does not reflect the Father's character or Yeshua's even a little bit.

The penalty for actual rape in the Torah is the death of the rapist, whereas the woman is declared guiltless.

## Divorce and Remarriage

*Deut 24:1-3 When a man hath taken a wife, and married her, and it come to pass that she find no favour in his eyes, because he hath found some uncleanness in her: then **let him write her a bill of divorcement, and give it in her hand, and send her out of his house.***

*And when she is departed out of his house, **she may go and be another man's wife.***

Contrary to what much of Christianity says, divorce is not the unforgivable sin. It is written that it is permitted; however, the woman must be set free legally. During Yeshua's time, men were just sending their wives away without a proper divorce and without any means of support. This was called "putting her away." She couldn't get a job, so she had three options (1) go home to her family, who might refuse to take her, (2) live with another man who will take care of her, making her an adulteress, or (3) become a prostitute. See now why Yeshua said that such men were responsible for making their wives adulteresses?

*Matt 5:31-32 It hath been said, Whosoever shall put away his wife, let him give her a writing of divorcement:*

*[32] But I say unto you, That **whosoever shall "put away" his wife**, saving for the cause of fornication, causeth her to commit adultery: and whosoever shall marry her that is "divorced" committeth adultery.*

Now, this is a really misleading translation. See verse 32? The phrase "put away" is the same Greek word apoloo'o as the one for "divorced" – but not the same as the word in vs 31 meaning divorcement, apostaseeon! No common root, no nothing. This verse was handled in such a way as to make it look like Messiah was overturning Torah when in fact He was upholding it. Let's look at verse 32 being consistent with the wording

*But I say unto you, That **whosoever shall put away his wife**, saving for the cause of fornication, causeth her to commit adultery: and **whosoever shall marry her that is put away committeth adultery**.*

This is consistent with Torah; any man who marries a married woman is definitely committing adultery! The only way a man is not responsible for making his wife an adulterer, by the act of putting her away, is the man whose wife is already an adulteress!

The only thing that was forbidden, and I call this the Elizabeth Taylor Clause, was if you divorced and remarried someone else, you cannot go back to your first husband ever again. It was absolutely forbidden.

*Deut 24:3-4 **And if the latter husband hate her, and write her a bill of divorcement**, and giveth it in her hand, and sendeth her out of his house; **or if the latter husband die**, which took her to be his wife; **Her former husband, which sent her away, may not take her again to be his wife**, after that she is defiled; for that is abomination before the L<small>ORD</small>: and thou shalt not cause the land to sin, which the L<small>ORD</small> thy God giveth thee for an inheritance.*

And this verse is the entire context of Romans 7, the great mystery of the gospel. YHVH called Israel His wife, but in Isaiah and Jeremiah He handed the Nation a bill of divorcement and the nation went off into paganism and "married" itself to other gods.[123] And yet He said, "Return to Me!"[124] It was the unanswerable question that confused the great sages for hundreds of years. How can YHVH take His adulterous wife back after she has been with someone else? The answer, He must die Himself and resurrect – becoming the eternal Bridegroom, the New Adam, and Israel the eternal Bride! Halleluyah! Hence Yeshua, YHVH in the flesh, had to die to take the penalty of His former wife's sins upon Himself.

---

[123] Is 50:1; Jer 3:8
[124] Ho 14:1

## Biblical Circumcision vs Pharisaic Circumcision

I debated about not going here, but I decided to go ahead and write about this.

First of all, it was not what they do in hospitals today – that is based on Pharisaic circumcision. This method of radical circumcision was instituted during the Greek occupation, when men were reversing their circumcisions (please don't ask me how, you probably don't want to know and if you do want to know, then you can research it yourself) in order to get into the gymnasiums. Before that time, they used to just take a bit of the skin off the top, maybe half the foreskin. What is done now is excessive. It was also done on the 8th day and not at birth, and although I won't go into it here, the human body has some amazing things that kick in on the 8th day that aid the healing process!

Pharisaic circumcision was also a rite performed when one decided to convert to Rabbinic Judaism, and if one did this, then they were required to follow the tenants of Judaism according to the traditions of the elders. As such, they would not be able to simply follow the Torah; they would be under the authority of the rabbis instead of Yeshua. This is why Paul made this statement.

*Gal 5:1-3 Stand fast therefore in the liberty wherewith Christ hath made us free, and be not entangled again with the yoke of bondage* (contained in the thousands of rabbinical decrees).

*Behold, I Paul say unto you, that if ye be* (Rabbinically) *circumcised, Christ shall profit you nothing* (because you will have to live according to Rabbinical instructions, not Yeshua's Torah).

*3For I testify again to every man that is* (Rabbinically) *circumcised, that he is a debtor to do the whole law* (oral law, now in written form as the Talmud).

To become circumcised by the ultra-strict House of Shammai (the circumcision group) was much the same as joining some churches I have been in. I once walked into a denomination where they had a list of 20 things I had to accept as true – things like pre-trib rapture – as well as things I was not allowed to believe. I wasn't even allowed to discuss them. In other words, leave your brains at the door and enter in to our bondage and say yes every time we say something is true. I also once went to a Messianic synagogue where I was told three or four things I was not allowed to believe or discuss! No one in this life has the right to tell you what you have to believe except for God. The Bible and the Holy Spirit are both incredible gifts, given to us to protect us from those who feel they have the right to impose their own standards and beliefs on us – when only our Master has the right to do it. Guard the freedom you have in Messiah and Torah, it is of greater worth than all the gold in the universe.

## A Start

You probably have more questions. I could have talked about piercings (allowed) and tattoos (forbidden), about murder and stealing and adultery, but all I wanted was to give you a firm starting place on some of the issues that there are big misconceptions about. I have no desire to cover everything, and that's where you and your beautiful God-given intellect come in. I want you to dig deep and learn this for yourself. I don't want you to ever say, "Well, Tyler says," because what I say isn't important – it's what Yeshua says and it's what is written in the Word, and not in any commentaries, that is your lifeline. That is the final authority, not me or any teacher, pastor, rabbi, evangelist – we are all just poor shadows of our King, knowing just enough to hopefully realize how little we really know. I have said it before and I will say it again, I am just a follower of the King doing my very best to faithfully represent Him and render honor to Him, but I will never arrive at a place where I can lay down the 100% absolute truth to anyone. Only One Man who was ever born of a woman could ever lay claim to that, and I assure you that isn't me.

My intention, from the first page, has not been to establish my own halakah for you to observe, because I do not have the authority to do that. I am not the Holy Spirit, neither am I inerrant. I told you what I know, and sometimes what I simply believe, to be true.

Your walk is not going to look exactly the same way mine does. You may very well decide not to eat milk and meat together and I won't criticize you – unless you try and force me to do it that way too. You may decide to incorporate some Jewish traditions, and again, this is just fine but not required. One of the things that is absolutely imperative in this walk is that we come to a place of unity, which is different than uniformity. Unity means we come together under a common King with a common goal, loving Him and one another and giving Him honor in the sight of the Nations. Uniformity means that we do everything exactly the same as everyone else, and the only way we can do that is by everyone agreeing to follow one human voice. Of course, this will never work, because too many men have no desire whatsoever to be ruled, even by God.  But a great many men desire to be that one voice everyone else is obeying.  I do not want that kind of responsibility.

Unity requires love, patience, humility and grace.  Unity says, "we agree on the really vital issues, let's trust God on the small stuff."  Uniformity is a conqueror, bent on domination -- to the man whose goal is uniformity, there are no small issues.

Which leads me to cover one more matter that can really derail us, and that matter is called "opinion."

## Common Troubles  – Calendars and Names and Paganism

When people learn that Torah is still alive and well and not nailed to the cross, there are some very discouraging and unfruitful traps they can fall into.  The first being Calendars and the second is "The Name Game" and the third I call "not everything is pagan for crying out loud!"

Throughout this book, I have presented it as though the calendar I keep (the one found in the Talmud) is correct, however I can't prove it because it is not absolutely spelled out in the Bible, and neither is anyone else's.  When things aren't written down **in "Thus saith the LORD" context**, I caution people not to get caught in a "camp," one way or another.  In fact, I suggest going by the rabbinical calendar until you have enough information to choose another, which you may never do, and that is fine with me.  It is not important to me the exact day you celebrate the Feasts on, only that you do celebrate them according to "a" calendar, as there is no "the" calendar at this time.  The rabbinical dates for Feasts are the ones you find on most secular calendars, or you can do an internet search for "Passover 2015" and find out what day they are celebrating on.  It makes it easier to get the day off of work if you can show it to your boss in writing.  Whatever calendar you choose, you will be taking someone's word for it, and not the Bible's.  People will go to great lengths to prove that their calendar is the one true calendar, but I am not going to do that to you.  Trust YHVH, do your best, and don't sweat the small stuff.

Another thing people get caught up in is how to pronounce YHVH.  And people get weird about that, even though Moses did not do us the favor of using a tape recorder at Mt Sinai.  So we don't know how to pronounce it with 100% certainty.  I think my way is probably right, just like everyone else thinks their way is probably right.  The only thing we know is that there is no J in Hebrew so it can't start with a J sound (which never existed until less than 400 years ago).  I hear a couple of different versions and since no one can prove it, it's just a big headache.  I stay away from divisive people and silly arguments.  It's just not worth it and detracts from growing in the Spirit.  It accomplishes absolutely nothing.  In fact, I won't even tell you the way I pronounce it, so that you have the freedom to explore it yourself.

Since my goal for you is to grow in obedience AND the Spirit, to the honor and glory of our King, it is my sincere wish to spare you from fruitless arguments.

The third area is paganism.   And yes, the mixing of what was given at Sinai with paganism is devastating, and we see it all through the Bible, even in the New Testament (or in Hebrew, B'rit Hadasha).  People become so very upset about even the possibility of doing anything pagan that they go searching for it, way beyond the obvious forms; sometimes causing damage and accomplishing nothing but starting uproar and causing confusion.  I like to focus on the truth, on the light, because I believe wholeheartedly that light exposes darkness and that truth exposes lies.  I don't want to wallow through the mud when I can instead delve into the truth.

One thing I hope, above all, is that you will not allow anyone to bully you in to doing things their way.  In fact, if I could give you one piece of advice it is this – carefully look at the fruit of the person who is trying to teach you.  Does their fruit line up with Gal 5:22-23 or are they far, far from it?  Because nothing we do or teach is worth a thing if we are not producing good fruit as a result of it.

Anyone who seeks to become your personal Holy Spirit is seeking to deprive you of a direct relationship with YHVH.  Everything that everyone says must be measured against the Word, regardless of how genuine they appear or convincing they sound, or whatever academic of genetic credentials they try to impress you with.

## The Fruit of the Spirit in Abundance

*Gal 5:22-23 But the fruit of the Spirit is love, joy, peace, longsuffering, gentleness, goodness, faith, meekness, temperance: against such there is no law.*

There is nothing in the written Torah against being the living embodiment of these qualities, as the verse points out.  In my experience, during for the first 12 years of my walk my fruit did not change much at all.  No amount of Bible reading touched my anger and resentment and pride. I was doing things that made church people happier because I acted somewhat differently on the outside, but on the inside I was mostly the same.  For the first 15 months of Torah, it didn't get much better, under a controlling, disapproving teacher.  I had more knowledge, but knowledge isn't everything.  Sometimes I wanted to give up entirely, but I knew it was the truth so I just couldn't.  Thankfully, I hooked up with a teacher who taught about the Torah and the fruit of the Spirit and over the last two years of my life I have undergone nothing less than a miraculous transformation; I am circumcising my heart.  I know I am because it hurts.  I am learning to love God and love my neighbor – through the Torah laws, which define the **basics** of what it looks like to love someone.  When I was making it up as I went along, or following church expectations, I was living as though they were my masters, but when I bent the knee and allowed the Master Yeshua to call all the shots, big things started happening.

It hasn't been easy – I had to learn to treat myself with grace so that I could extend it to others.  I had to see myself as one of the children of Israel, not a teenager, not a grownup, but a child. Once I did that, I was able to cut myself a lot of slack and I could fail and repent without feeling like a hopeless failure.  This is still a new and wondrous world for me, one I pray you will desire to be a part of, the Covenants of promise that all belong to you. They have for a long time now, but you and I and

251

the people who taught us were robbed of it generations ago. It's time to seize our inheritance and run with it, to fill our lamps with oil. I am writing this book because I didn't have anything like it, and because I want to glorify God by restoring His reputation among people who have not heard the whole story about Him. I want this to be a starting place for you, not your final destination. I don't want you to struggle as much as I did, I don't want you to be as discouraged as I was and I don't want you to give up when people tell you that you have fallen from grace. Because when you share this with them, they are going to see it from the viewpoint of themselves being perceived as wrong, their lives being judged. That is the natural and normal reaction. I was praying about this once and the following came to me about the parable of the sower -

"Who are the birds who snatch the seeds of the Word away from our path before they can take root? Sadly, the very ones we invite to take a look at the seed.

How many of us have been trained, carefully trained, when we receive something new -- to take it to a Pastor, Rabbi, or advisor before taking it to YHVH and going and seeking in the Word and meditating upon it? If I share something with my Pastor that he isn't already teaching, 99% of the time he/she is going to do their best to discredit it. If I go to an anti-missionary to find out if Yeshua is Messiah, they are going to their best to discredit Him. I am of the tendency to believe that we gravitate towards the people who are going to tell us what we want to believe, and if what we want is the truth, we will gravitate towards Him first and foremost instead of men. The Bereans didn't ask their Rabbi if Paul was teaching truth, they went to the Tanakh, the Old Testament scriptures, to see what was written by Moses and the Prophets.

We show exactly what we desire to believe by whose counsel we pursue. We all need to be wise like the Berean Jews and decide to believe the whole Word or we most certainly will follow after men, to our destruction."

I don't want you to trust me. I want you to search the Word to see if what I am saying is true. I won't be beside you on Judgment Day, because I will be answering for myself. I want you to be a Berean, for your sake. Everything I have written is for His glory and for your sake. I have no congregation, I collect no tithes, I have no power base to establish, and I don't see any of that ever changing as I have no desire to ever do any of those things.

Before I close this out, I want to tell you something very important –

*Yeshua and the Torah should never be used as a bludgeon to try and change others, but as a tool to change ourselves. If you are intent on changing others, you have missed the point entirely. This is about your holiness, your sanctification, your relationship with God. But most of all, this is about Him and Who He is and How He deserves to be glorified through His people.*

If I had one thing to beg of you – besides what I have already asked, which is to search out the scriptures to find out if I am telling the truth, it would be to never forget where you came from, and to never despise the people who are still there.

## Burning the Bridge Behind You – A Parable About Mercy and the Pursuit of Truth

A man in a land of great darkness saw a bridge leading off over a chasm into an unseen land. The slats of the bridge were the right size for a man's foot and even though the first step was very dark indeed, it contained a bit of light so he placed his foot upon it. The next step was perceptibly lighter, and in fact he realized that he could look ahead and see more and more light and less darkness. It was hard leaving the comfortable familiarity of the darkness he knew, especially since his family remained back in the darkness, but the light was drawing him and so he continued, one step at a time, each time making the choice to leave some of the darkness behind and step into new light.

After some time, he became very impressed and puffed up with the amount of light he was walking in, and the amount of darkness he had trodden under his feet. He stopped and turned around and much to his horror all he could see was a path of increasing darkness. Facing backwards, he became contemptuous of that darkness and decided to focus his efforts on destroying it, ignoring the faint cries from those further on to turn around and keep going. So he removed a lighter from his pocket and kindled a fire on the slats that had previously been behind him, thinking to exterminate the darkness he saw. The fire quickly began consuming that ancient path that had led into the light, even destroying the guard rails. The man delighted in the destruction of the darkness, never giving a thought to the people on the dark end of the chasm, or those further back on the path -- or, to the fact that he was not yet safely to the other side of the chasm. In his arrogance and contempt, he fell to destruction, never having reached his destination, and destroyed the path for many.

This is the tragedy of the Protestant Reformation, the Charismatic movement, the Hebrew Roots Movement, etc....

The darkness was the darkness the man was born into spiritually. The bridge is the calling of YHVH out of that darkness through restoration in Yeshua Messiah, but he did not know them by those names at first, he knew God and Jesus. The slats represent truth to walk in and lies to trample underfoot. Step by step he went forward, coming more and more out of the darkness and into more and more light until the splendid awareness of his knowledge got the better of him and he turned his back on God without even realizing it, in order to gaze upon darkness instead of upon the light. Facing the wrong direction, he no longer had the perspective to see the mercy of a path growing ever more illuminated, but instead all he could see was a path getting darker. Contempt filled his heart and he cared nothing for the people on what he perceived as a path of darkness; he had no love for them, no compassion, but instead only impatience. From his vantage point, he did not see the truth, that they were now on the path of light, and that he had turned away from that light and was now on the path of darkness. He deceived himself into thinking he was destroying the path to sin, but in actuality he was destroying mercy -- the message of the Torah and the Prophets, the slats and the guard rails of the bridge that is Messiah. Having no mercy to stand on, he fell and took others with him, ignoring the cries of those further along down the road to repent and turn back to God.

It is human nature to believe we have arrived, to take our eyes off the prize and become more focused on the deception than on the truth. We start out in such deception, "our fathers have inherited lies" (Jer 16:19) and we get a bit of truth and it is a great temptation to turn around and view those lies with contempt. If that contempt is greater than our desire for truth, we will not turn back around. There is a difference between glancing back over your shoulder to offer encouragement to those behind you and turning around and facing the opposite direction. I see people completely derailed by the idea that it is their personal ministry to expose lies -- in fact it's all I ever see them do and they are out in droves on Facebook. They are so intent on burning the bridge (interesting that I wrote bride first) behind them that they forget that the point of the bridge is to lead someone out of falsehood.  It is a step by step process, there are no shortcuts. Lies must be personally confronted one by one -- as King Josiah showed us, the idols had to be destroyed from the land one at a time. As Joshua and Caleb showed us, the enemies must be killed or driven out one by one, town by town, and we don't dare turn around like Lot's wife because when we focus on the deception, on the sin, on what is behind us, forgetting to press on in endurance, it is then that we are overcome.

So you know the Name of Yeshua and YHVH, you know some Torah, you're Spirit baptized, you know the Gospel that Messiah preached, you know some things about the book of Revelation -- do not become so impressed with these things that you stop striving forward. Going forward takes far more humility and love than turning around with a sneer on your face. As you go forward, call an encouraging word over your shoulder so that people in darkness can hear and find the path, but don't think you can stand your ground, facing in the wrong direction, and do anything other than hold people up. Do not dare to trample upon the mercy given you (and that path *is* the mercy of God). Do not destroy the path for others. Do not despise the path! You did not create the path, and so it is not yours to destroy. No one gets to the other side of the chasm in this lifetime, and so we need to keep going forward.

I am going to conclude all this with my mini-statement of faith and the letter I wrote this year to all my friends and family. I finally felt mature and knowledgeable enough to share it with them just this past spring. I wish you peace, or as Yeshua would say, Shalom. You are in my prayers.

## Who Am I? – My Statement of Faith

One of the first questions I asked in this book was "Who am I?" I'd like to expand upon my answer now, with something I wrote a while back --

I am not a Jew. I was not born a Jew. I am not trying to be a Jew. I will never be a Jew. Jewish traditions hold no allure for me whatsoever. It is wonderful to be a Jew -- but I was not made to be one.

I was born of the Nations. I was called out from the Nations, by a God who designed me to be from the Nations, to speak one of the languages of the Nations, so I could be His in full view of the Nations. I make no apologies for being from the Nations, nor should I!

What I am is grafted into the olive tree of Israel; not of the Jews, and no longer of the Gentiles. I am called to obey the laws of the people of Israel, the Torah, not the laws of the Jews (Talmud), or walk in the ways of the Gentiles (paganism and humanism), or the laws of the Church (denominational doctrines and traditions).

I am not trying to be a Jew. I am not trying to be a Gentile. I am trying to be an Israelite. Because I come from the Nations, I will never look Jewish to a Jew, although to the untrained eye, it might appear so because I will do some of the things that they do, the way they do it, but other things I will do in a way that looks utterly foreign to them. And that's okay.

I look this way because I am a person who was called out of the Nations, by the Master Yeshua the Messiah of Israel, to be a part of His people, obeying His laws, and waiting for His return. I am doing my best, and it's going to look weird to people, but that's where patience and compassion come into the picture. I have to obey the Torah of YHVH, but the way I obey it doesn't have to look exactly the same as the way you obey it.

Torah is a pursuit and a journey of a child with its Father. As each child is individually unique, so will our walk with the Father be unique. Same rules for all the children, born Jewish or born of the Nations, but at different points along the walk, we will be better and worse than others at figuring out how to live in obedience. And it's okay for those of us from the Nations to look strange; we weren't raised like this. It's a struggle and a learning process. We are wild olive branches receiving nourishment from the root of Israel, and learning to thrive.  We will fail all the time; start expecting failure and realize that after 3500 years, we are all doing it wrong, but love spurs us on to try anyway -- and faith tells us that YHVH greatly rejoices in our pursuit of obedience.

Who am I?  A woman greater than I will ever be said it beautifully.  I am just "a mother in Israel."[125]

---

[125] Judges 5:7

## My Testimony to My Friends and Family About Torah

About a month before starting to write this book, I was getting ready to send out the twins' pictures and I was prompted to write this letter about what we believe and why. I wanted to clear up any misconceptions that we had become Jewish or that our faith in Messiah's work was lacking in any way and so here it is. Feel free to rewrite it and use it if it helps you. It's a pretty quick summation of what I discussed in the rest of the book –

Almost three years ago, our family went through an amazing change that I want to share with you. Back in June of 2011 we were watching an online religious conference and I heard the voice of the LORD challenge me, "Please tell me where in scripture it says you can eat pork." I was kind of shocked; it was absolutely out of nowhere. I went to my Bible and started pulling out the verses I used to justify it, and studied them in context and I was very upset to find that they had nothing to do with eating pork at all, that I had been taking them out of context all my life, and I was further shocked to find that one very misleading verse was added by translators (the parenthetical statement in Mark 7:19) to make the eating of pork look like it was now acceptable.

I found out that the word food (when applied to meat) was defined in the Bible in Leviticus 11, and that any sort of meat anywhere in scripture that was called food fell within those guidelines, nothing else qualified. I discovered that Acts 10 wasn't about eating unclean at all, but about two rabbinical laws (ones not found in the writings of Moses, being the books of Genesis through Deuteronomy) – the first being that any clean animal that touched an unclean animal was now unfit for eating ("Peter rise and eat" meant it was okay to eat the clean animals even though they were in contact with unclean animals), and the second being the first century belief that any Gentile who had not undergone full conversion to rabbinic Judaism (meaning they submit to the traditions of the elders, like ritual hand washing, the washing of cups, pots and tables, and the additional restrictions they made for the Sabbath – found today recorded in the Talmud) was unclean if they were not keeping Torah and common if they were keeping Torah. According to Rabbinical law, Peter could not come in contact with Gentiles who had not converted to Judaism, and he certainly could not eat with them or go into their houses. If I had read to the end of the chapter, I would have seen that his vision was about people, not about eating things that the Bible says are not food, but I believed what I had always been taught.

We were very shocked, but we gave up all our pork and Mark and the boys gave up all seafood that did not have fins and scales (I was already allergic to shellfish). Three weeks later, I noticed that I had not had a single asthma attack; I also noticed that my fingers didn't hurt anymore and they had started to untwist, and my blood pressure was normal. I found that out when I finally went in to renew my prescription that I had let lapse a few weeks earlier.

At this point, we knew we had to figure out what was going on, and we were in for another shock. We found that the early church, the same Body that worked miracles and raised people from the dead, kept the seventh day Sabbath and that the church as a whole did not change that until ordered to by Rome centuries later. None of the early disciples of Yeshua (Jesus' real name) would have ever worshiped on Sunday as Sabbath and none of them did – we know this from the writings of the earliest church fathers and from other historical writings. We read what the Bible said about Sabbath and decided that in order to follow Yeshua, we needed to do what He did – because as He said, "My doctrine is not my own, but Him that sent Me" -- John 7:16. In fact, in reading the only scriptures that the apostles ever had, the Old Testament, we found out how incredibly important Sabbath is to God, that it is an affirmation that we believe He created the world in six days and then rested on the seventh, and that it is also an affirmation of our belief that Messiah will return after 6,000 years of human rule upon this earth and reign for 1,000 when He will give us rest from our labors. We also found out that the New Testament reference to the "Lord's Day" didn't mean Sunday – but instead what was referred to in both the Old Testament and the New as the Day of the LORD – the time of wrath to come upon the whole world. This is exactly what Revelation was referring to when speaking of being in the Spirit on the LORD's Day -- John was prophetically experiencing the unveiling of the Tribulation.

The next change we made was to keep the Feasts in Lev 23, just like our Savior and His disciples always did, including Paul. In fact, Paul was in Jerusalem for the Feast (we see from Acts 20:6 that the Passover had just been kept and they were heading to Jerusalem for Shavuot) when this came up in Acts 21:18-24

*And the day following Paul went in with us unto James; and all the elders were present. And when he had saluted them, he declared particularly what things God had wrought among the Gentiles by his ministry. And when they heard it, they glorified the Lord, and said unto him, Thou seest, brother, how many thousands of Jews there are which believe; and **they are all zealous for the law**: and they are informed of thee, that thou teachest all the Jews which are among the Gentiles to forsake Moses, saying that they ought not to circumcise their children, neither to walk after the customs. What is it therefore? the multitude must needs come together: for they will hear that thou art come. Do therefore this that we say to thee: We have four men which have a vow on them; them take, and purify thyself with them, and be at charges with them, that they may shave their heads: and all may know that those things, whereof they were informed concerning thee, are nothing; but that **thou thyself also walkest orderly, and keepest the law.***

I don't know how I didn't see it for so many years of Bible reading, but I didn't. Paul didn't teach the Gentiles not to follow the law, he didn't teach people not to have their sons circumcised (in fact he himself had Timothy circumcised in Acts 16:3). And Paul himself kept the law. Otherwise, James would have been telling Paul to lie about what he was doing.

So we traded Christmas for Sukkot, the true birth of Messiah during the Feast of Tabernacles, which is a shadow picture of Him coming back to reign for a thousand years. When we keep that feast, we are making a declaration that we believe He was, is, and is coming. We keep Yom Kippur, which is a declaration that we believe that Yeshua is the salvation of the Nation of Israel as a whole, that "all Israel shall be saved." We keep Yom Teruah, the Day of Trumpets, which occurs on "the day and hour that no man knows" at the sighting of the first sliver of the new moon during the 7th biblical month of Tishri. We traded Pentecost for Shavuot, the prophetic shadow picture of the Spirit being poured out on the assembly, as we see in the book of Acts, just as the Law was given at Mt Sinai to the assembly, which according to Stephen was the true birth of the church (Acts 7:38) – not in Jerusalem, but at Sinai. We also traded Easter for Passover, the shadow picture of Messiah coming to die to restore us to right standing with God, in order to obey Him when He said, "from now on, do this in remembrance of Me." We traded Resurrection Sunday for First Fruits, the feast which served as a shadow of Messiah rising up out of the earth and ascending to be presented as a holy offering to the Father. In Leviticus 23, these are called the Feasts of the LORD, and were to be celebrated by His people Israel forever, not just the Jews, but all those who are in covenant with Him. Just like at Mt Sinai, the descendants of Jacob plus the mixed multitude who came out of Egypt.

We learned from I John 3:4 that sin is defined as transgression of the law. I John 1:10 says that if we claim we do not sin we are liars, so sin still exists, and that was written long after the death of the other apostles, including Paul. I read what Peter said about Paul in 2 Peter 3:15-16 – that his writings were hard to understand and easily twisted. And I began to see that Peter was right because the more I understood what everyone besides Paul was saying, the more I realized that the only way I could justify what I had been doing was with Paul's writings. I couldn't use Yeshua (Jesus), Moses, John, Peter or any of the others to back up any of the doctrines I was taught – I had to ignore Yeshua almost entirely, or take Him out of context. I decided that Yeshua, and not Paul, died for me, so I had to give weight to what Yeshua said first and foremost. He said this.

*Matt 5:17-19* **Think not that I am come to destroy the law, or the prophets: I am not come to destroy, but to pleroo**. *For verily I say unto you, Till heaven and earth pass, one jot or one tittle shall in no wise pass from the law, till all be fulfilled. Whosoever therefore shall break one of these least commandments, and shall teach men so, he shall be called the least in the kingdom of heaven: but* **whosoever shall do and teach them, the same shall be called great in the kingdom of heaven**.

I studied and found that pleroo did not mean fulfill as in "do away with." It can mean many things, but never that. It means to confirm, fill up, perform – and when Paul uses that word in Roman 15:19 – it means fully preach. This is exactly what Yeshua did in the verses that followed. Not only did He fully preach the law, He brought fuller meaning to it, making it more honest and removing the loopholes the some of the religious leaders had added with their rabbinical rulings (extra laws). He said right in the passage I quoted that whoever breaks even a small law and teaches others to do so will be least, but those who teach the law and keep it will be great. Why would He teach that about the Kingdom of Heaven if He was going to destroy the law? What He destroyed was the debt of sin which we were condemned by. He took the penalty, but nowhere does it say that He kept the Father's commandments so that we don't have to.  As we can see around us, Heaven and Earth have not passed, and all of the prophecies of the Bible have not come to pass!  He said, "Follow Me."  Indeed how can we follow Him if we do not live as He lived?

I pray you are still reading, because I love you, and it is my greatest fear that no one will ever share this with you.  I love you so much that I am willing to have you never speak to me again just in the hopes that this will help you come closer to our God.

Yeshua had much to say about law breaking, and how serious it is.  Right after warning about false prophets and their fruits, Yeshua said this in Matthew 7:21-23

*Not every one that saith unto me, Lord, Lord, shall enter into the kingdom of heaven;* **but he that doeth the will of my Father** *which is in heaven. Many will say to me in that day, Lord, Lord, have we not prophesied in thy name? and in thy name have cast out devils? and in thy name done many wonderful works? And then will I profess unto them, I never knew you: depart from me,* **ye that work iniquity**.

It is not enough to confess Him as Lord, we have to do the will of His Father in Heaven in order to make Him Lord, and the will of His Father was given at Sinai, so that we would be set apart from the rest of the world by obedience to His way of life, the laws given to Moses.  These people in this passage were doing amazing works, but they were working iniquity, the Greek word anomia, which means "lawlessness" – they were living apart from the laws of God.  There is no distinction between Jew and Gentile here, and as we saw before Paul was not teaching the Gentiles to not keep Torah.  The Acts 15 council decided that in order to enter in to the body of believers, Gentiles had to first commit to 4 changes in their lives and then they could learn the rest of the Torah, Acts 15:21

*For Moses of old time hath in every city them that preach him, being read in the synagogues every sabbath day.*

What we were taught were our only requirements were simply the minimum requirements to be able to enter into the synagogue – because those 4 requirements were about what happens in pagan temples – sex with cult prostitutes, blood drinking, animals strangled for sacrifice, and association with idols. If those are the only requirements, then we would be permitted to do absolutely anything that is not on the list.  But from the beginning of the church at Sinai, there has only been one law for Jew and Gentile – Ex 12:49 (as well as many other references).

*One law shall be to him that is homeborn, and unto the stranger that sojourneth among you.*

As Paul said, there is no wall of division, the same standards always applied to everyone equally.  Ephesians 2:11-21

*Wherefore remember, that ye **being in time past Gentiles** in the flesh, who are called Uncircumcision* (not official converts to Judaism) *by that which is called the Circumcision in the flesh made by hands* (those submitted to rabbinical Judaism); *that **at that time ye were without Christ, being aliens from the commonwealth of Israel, and strangers from the covenants*** (plural, meaning all former covenants still apply) *of promise, having no hope, and without God in the world: but now in Christ Jesus ye who sometimes were far off are made nigh by the blood of Christ.  For he is our peace, who hath made both one, and **hath broken down the middle wall of partition between us; having abolished in his flesh the enmity, even the law of commandments contained in ordinances*** (rabbinical ordinances that kept Jews and Gentiles apart, and by definition, kept Gentiles from being able to come to the gospel); *for to make in himself of twain one* *new man, so making peace; and that he might reconcile both unto God in one body by the cross, having slain the enmity thereby: and came and preached peace to you which were afar off, and to them that were nigh. for through him we both have access by one Spirit unto the Father. Now therefore **ye are no more strangers and foreigners, but fellow citizens with the saints** (of the nation of Israel, same exact standards), **and of the household of God**; and are built upon the foundation of the apostles and prophets, Jesus Christ himself being the chief corner stone; in whom all the building fitly framed together groweth unto an holy temple in the Lord: in whom ye also are builded together for an habitation of God through the Spirit.*

The word holy is not really understood by most people, but it means "set apart." It means different, and the opposite of set apart is common. If we live like the world does in any way, it would be remarked what we have in common with them, but we are supposed to be set apart, and how we are set apart is by striving to live as Messiah lived, and He was a Torah keeping Jewish Rabbi. In fact, if Yeshua had broken even one of the laws given by God to Moses on Mt Sinai, according to I John 3:4, He would have been a sinner and we would be dead in our sins. If He added or took away from the law in any way, He would have broken Deut 4:2 and 12:32, and we would be dead in our sins.

What did our Savior say about Moses' writings? John 5:46-47

*For **had ye believed Moses, ye would have believed me**: for he wrote of me. But **if ye believe not his writings, how shall ye believe my words?***

Yeshua says that if we do not believe Moses, we will not believe what He says, and we were taught not to believe Moses. We are taught that when God told Moses "forever" over and over and over again, that He really just meant, for another 1400 years or so. We were taught that

Moses created the laws, but over and over again it says, *"And the LORD said, "Speak to the children of Israel and tell them..."* Moses prophesied the coming One of Israel. Moses was so beloved of God that He spoke to him face to face as a man speaks with his friend (Ex 33:11), and so I believe with my whole heart that whatever Moses says is absolutely true. Moses said this in Deut 30 after speaking the law once more to the children of Israel before his death.

Deut 30:11-16 *For this commandment which I command thee this day, it is not hidden from thee, neither is it far off. t is not in heaven, that thou shouldest say, Who shall go up for us to heaven, and bring it unto us, that we may hear it, and do it? Neither is it beyond the sea, that thou shouldest say, Who shall go over the sea for us, and bring it unto us, that we may hear it, and do it? But the word **is very nigh unto thee, in thy mouth, and in thy heart, that thou mayst do it** See, I have set before thee this day life and good, and death and evil; in that **I command thee this day to love the Lord thy God, to walk in his ways, and to keep his commandments and his statutes and his judgments,** that thou mayest live and multiply: and the Lord thy God shall bless thee in the land whither thou goest to possess it.*

Verse 16 tells us how to love God, by walking in His ways through the keeping his commandments, statutes and judgments. He said that it is not out of reach, or impossible; that it is in our hearts. There is no reference to ceremonial law, in fact, you will never find that phrase anywhere in the Bible (for that matter you will never find the words legalism, Judaizer, or the phrase spiritual Israel either). Yeshua said this exact same thing in John 14:15, equating Himself with the lawgiver at Sinai.

*"If you love Me, you will keep my commandments."*

Some people say He was only referring to two of them, love God with all your heart, mind and strength (Deut 6:5) and love your neighbor (Lev 19:18) but He said elsewhere that all of the other commandments are part and parcel with these, inseparable and connected.

*Matt 22:40 On these two commandments hang all the law and the prophets.*

We love God and make Him our God by living according to what He says is good and bad. Mal 3:6 – He never changes, not ever. Bad never becomes good and good never becomes bad, or it makes him a liar, like a mere man. His word is eternal or temporary, true or false, life or death.

One closing thing, does Yeshua ever once say that the law has been done away with? Wouldn't He have said it? Doesn't it take a "thus saith the LORD" to undo a "Thus saith the LORD?" What did He say? What are His last words as recorded by Matthew? Matthew 28:18-20

*And Jesus came and spake unto them, saying, All power is given unto me in heaven and in earth. Go ye therefore, and teach **all nations**, baptizing them in the name of the Father, and of the Son, and of the Holy Ghost: **<u>teaching them to observe all things whatsoever I have commanded you</u>**: and, lo, I am with you always, even unto the end of the world. Amen.*

He just said that all power is given to Him in Heaven and on Earth, and He did not say "You are free from the law." He said, in a nutshell, what He had been saying all along, "Keep my commandments and teach others to do the same." If He taught anything before His death that diminished the commandments, again, He would be a sinner and we are dead in our sins. If He had ever taught against the law or broke it, they

would not have needed false witnesses at His trial.  Was He a sinner?
May it never be!

I pray my words are received with the love in which they are given, I
know this is hard, but the last few years have been so fulfilling for us,
we have the whole of scriptures, the eternal Word of God, as a gift for
all of us to teach us what is and is not acceptable to God. We keep it
because we love Him.  It is how He desires to be loved and worshiped,
not only in spirit, but also in truth.  We have not fallen from grace; we
have found it at last!

*Psalm 119:142* **Thy righteousness is an everlasting righteousness,
and thy law is the truth.**

All of my hopes and prayers for a full life in our Messiah go with you, that you may know my joy – the faith once delivered to our fathers.  I pray with all my heart, mind and being that this book has served as a bridge across the muddied waters of tradition and time – leading you to the fullness of Yeshua and Torah.  Don't stay on the bridge, whatever you do.  Keep moving.

I invite you to join me on my journey through my blog, where I explore God's revealed character through both Scripture and His Messiah.

http://theancientbridge.com/

## About The Cover

When Tyler asked me to do a painting for her book cover, my first thought was "It is not in me". But then again I am brought to remembrance of Joseph's story when he said the same thing. So I began to pray and asked for a copy of the book to read. There is a tremendous amount of labor that goes into writing a book. The scripture references, the editing, the hours of rereads and it is all for you! I was stirred to paint something inviting...something vivid...something that would draw the reader into the journey.

It is not coincidence that Tyler and I met, nor is it coincidence that I locked onto the words she has been writing for a while now. She has created a spiritual bridge with the stories and truth YHVH has given her; a bridge to cross over and do so on a foundation that is solid. I started with the bridge, knowing it had to be firm but also distinctive. It is not an ordinary bridge, not one someone finds every day; it's an extraordinary bridge. It will look foreign to us in many ways, but it is sure and it is the ancient path across unstable water. She did an amazing job of simplifying things while keeping the stones rigidly in place for they cannot be altered or moved. These stones are cut and formed by the Creator Himself and her ability to recognize this is amazing. The tree offers two things; shade from the direct light and food which nourishes the soul. She has achieved the balance of grace and truth, the most valuable part of our journey.

The reflections in the water I left murky with reddish tones because they are 'not quite' reflections of the One who is leading us. When we look down instead of up, we are more susceptible to deception and confusion. The bridge still supports us and the tree calls us forward nevertheless. The stones are catching some of the reflective light, but not enough to take our focus off the tree. There are delightful surprises along the way (if we have the vision to see them that way). The wildflowers and the appearance of growth continue to give us hope and longing to move forward. The bridge leads us to the tree and our purpose as Israel. Once we are there, we understand our journey like never before. Yet, it is a journey where we never really arrive.

Like the golden wheat ready for harvest, our very being is surrounded by the joy of light, touched by the warmth of the Son and prepare us to bow down in honor of Him, Our True King. There is delight in seeing all these things, but we also understand that the path has led to Him, Our true Messiah and all glory (even the light dancing on the wheat) belongs to Him.

I am honored and humbled by this opportunity, but what I have created is only an invitation. What I could illustrate and paint is only a small part of the complete picture. This book is a labor of love between a bride and her Bridegroom. I hope and pray you will understand its value and take time to embrace the words within it. I know they will spark new hope to continue the journey regardless of the obstacles, hold fast to the things that are important and meet some new friends along the way.

Darlene Dine

http://mytransparentjourneybydarlenedine.blogspot.com/